What People Are Saying About *Clear Minds & Dirty Feet*:

"It is a difficult task to make a book on apologetics engaging for the average reader. Well I'm very happy to say that Jon Morrison has done exactly that with his new book *Clear Minds & Dirty Feet*. It is at the same time delightful and full of interesting, cutting-edge content. A big thumbs up from me!"

Craig J. Hazen, Ph.D.
Director, MA Christian Apologetics Program at Biola University
Author of *Five Sacred Crossings*

There were two very impressive things that I noticed immediately when I picked up a copy of Jon Morrison's book, *Clear Minds & Dirty Feet*. The first was the last two words of the title: Dirty Feet. The second was the subtitle: A Reason to Hope, A Message to Share. In both title as well as subtitle, the author seemed to be making the same move: Christianity is first of all about believing certain truths, among these the Gospel itself. Morrison spends about ten chapters on this theme as well as answering objections. Then second, Christians are never supposed to leave it there, because Christianity is a lifestyle, a call to commitment. Morrison goes on to emphasize this message, too. As he states, Christianity is a call to get our feet dirty. That one-two movement of belief followed by doing something about it is at the center of Christianity. I encourage you to take a look at this volume.

Dr. Gary R. Habermas, Distinguished Research Professor & Chair, Dept. of Philosophy, Liberty University & Baptist Theological Seminary

"Christians need to learn how to reasonably defend and lovingly articulate their faith more than ever before. *Clear Minds & Dirty Feet* is a well-researched book that makes some tough issues both understandable and applicable to life. This is an enjoyable and much-needed book!"

Dr. Sean McDowell
Speaker, Author, Teacher at Biola University

"Jon Morrison is an excellent communicator. With clarity, humour, and insight, Jon shows the reasonableness of the Christian faith, dealing capably with the most common objections. His ability to break down difficult concepts into everyday street-level language makes this a valuable book for Christians and skeptics alike."

Steve Kroeker
Lead Pastor, Tsawassen Alliance Church

"I am thrilled about this book. Jon's wit, insight, cartoons and ready made analogies bring clarity to the difficult questions of faith that believers and unbelievers wrestle with. I highly recommend this book as a much needed and very beneficial resource."

Chris Price
Lead Pastor, Calvary Baptist Church

"This is a unique, much needed and well written analysis of important issues concerning Christianity. Jon is a wordsmith, cartoonist, and excellent apologist throughout the pages of this book. I would unreservedly recommend this book as great resource for anyone."

Chris Throness
Executive Pastor, Coquitlam Alliance Church

Clear Minds & Dirty Feet: A Reason To Hope, A Message To Share

Published By: Apologetics Canada Publishing.
Abbotsford, BC
Canada.

©2013 by Jon Morrison

ISBN-13: 978-1482778663

Some names have been changed to protect identities.

ACKNOWLEDGMENTS

I have leaned heavily on the works of others for this book. I am thankful to my friends who are gifted apologists. Them being in my life has made all the difference. I think of Chris Price, Andy Steiger, Chris Throness and my classmates in Oxford. I would like to thank the faculty at the *University of Biola* and the *Oxford Center For Christian Apologetics* for their conviction to train up a new generation of Christian apologists. No doubt, I have used many of your quotes or analogies. For that, I sincerely thank you for the help.

I would be nothing without the help of my family. I think of my mom, Patti; my dad, Dan; Matt, Chelsea and of course, Hayley. You are the greatest cheerleaders. Thank you for believing in me in all of life's ups and downs. I am so thankful to those who helped me out with the ever laborious work of editing, Evy Vanderhoek, Andrew MacDonald, Sally Start and Joan Newton.

I would also like to thank Nick Johnson or *HeyYou Media* for his help on the covers. Check out his amazing work at: heyyoumedia.com.

This being the fourth book I have written, I will never cease to thank Jesus for the ability to study, write and the time to actually put it all in a book. Even further, I thank Jesus for giving me life, saving me from my sins, rising to give me hope and orchestrating my life story to include having the chance to write books.

TABLE OF CONTENTS

		Page
1	Introduction: How Clear Minds Make Dirty Feet	10
2	Examining Your Worldview: What to Build a Life On	17
3	Faith and Science: What All The Fuss is About	29
4	The Evidence for God Part One: A Finely-Tuned Universe	57
5	The Evidence for God Part Two: The Big Banger	72
6	The Evidence for God Part Three: Objective Morality	84
7	Application Break: The Difference God Makes	94
8	The Bible: Why We Can Trust What God Says	96
9	This is Jesus: The Man Who Was Also God	116
10	The Hell Chapter: How God is Love but Not All Will Be Saved	136
11	The Resurrection of Jesus: The Day that Changed Everything	155
12	The Problem Of Evil: Whose Problem Is It?	176
13	Where Is God When It Hurts? Finding Light in Our Darkest Of Days	191
14	The Beauty of a Messenger's Feet	206
	Appendix: Giving Your Life to Jesus	211

FOREWORD

Every missionary knows that if you want to communicate, you need to know two things: the language and the culture. It can be easy to assume we know the language and culture of the people we are seeking to reach with the gospel. Often we don't. I was reminded of this recently while teaching a World Religions Course at a local Bible college. I began the class by asking for a volunteer. Taking the seat of the student, I asked the young man, who at this point was wishing he hadn't volunteered, to share the Gospel with the class. I then encouraged the class to listen carefully and to ask questions and challenge the student on anything he said. So as to temper the class, I instructed them that, upon finishing, the student would get to pick the next person to present. The next two minutes were a beautiful train wreck. In fact, it was a consistent theme throughout the semester as we began every class this way. The student's poor understanding of the Gospel and inability to communicate and defend its message spoke volumes about the current condition of many people in the church. That day after class the student thanked me for showing him how much he had to learn.

It's one thing to hear the Gospel and something completely different to understand its message, clearly articulate it and completely defend it. However, if the church in the West is going to be effective, we need to know the language and the culture of our community and time. We need to become better communicators of life's most important message – the Gospel. That's exactly what this book will help you do. As a Christian apologist, I have seen an unprecedented hunger in young people today asking questions like, "What is the meaning of life?"; "How can we know if God exists?"; "Is there life after death?" and many others. In order to reach this culture, Christians must be prepared to answer their questions in such a way that they can understand the Gospel. This requires that we deeply know the message. The effect of this is not only men and women able to communicate but having a desire to do so. When you grasp the beauty and hope of the Gospel you are compelled to tell others.

At *Apologetics Canada* we work hard to help churches engage both the skeptic and the believer. Our goal is to point people not just to truth but to the one who claimed and demonstrated to be Truth. As disciples or students of Jesus we need to have clear minds that lead to dirty feet.

I first met Jon Morrison when we teamed up to run the first *Apologetics Canada Conference* back in 2010. I was impressed with Jon's love for Jesus and the church. His ministry was doing what many were struggling to accomplish: keeping young adults and bringing new ones into the church. Having enjoyed a great deal of success in our first year together, God led us to unite our efforts. Jon has become my brother, friend and partner in this important ministry of doing Christian apologetics in Canada.

There has never been a more important time for students of Jesus to love people, speak truth and defend our hope. That is why I wholeheartedly endorse this book. Jon helps you articulate the Gospel and equips you to engage with the important questions of our culture using his unique wit, creativity and life experience.

Wherever you are at in life, as you wrestle with the contents of this book, I hope that your search is satisfied with a deeper love for the author of life – Jesus Christ.

-Andy Steiger
Director of Apologetics Canada
Author of "Thinking: Answering Life's Five Biggest Questions"

INTRODUCTION:
HOW CLEAR MINDS
MAKE DIRTY FEET

"People say to me continuously, 'Where is your God?'"

-Psalm 42:3

Erica was an honour roll student who was popular, beautiful and talented. Having grown up in the church, Erica loved Jesus with all her heart. Growing up in a broken home, Erica had some deeply ingrained doubts and questions about God. What if Christianity weren't the only true religion? If God is good, why does he not show up when I need him? Can the God of the Bible actually be trusted with my future?

After graduating from the youth program I was pastoring, Erica confessed to me that she often felt inferior when her faith was challenged by her peers in university. She felt like she was bullied intellectually both inside and out of the classroom. It frustrated Erica that she was not sure if there was an intellectual foundation to the faith she grew up believing.

Aware that Erica was not the only one struggling with these kinds of doubts, my friend Andy and I held an apologetics conference in Vancouver, BC. Andy called up speakers from all over North America who gave timely lectures on specific topics. It was one lecture, given by Dr. Craig Hazen from *Biola University,* on the "Evidence For The Resurrection Of Jesus" that became a turning point in Erica's life and an anchor for her faith.

In Dr. Hazen's lecture, Erica's eyes were opened to the overwhelming evidence in favour of the historical claim that Jesus had risen from the dead. She walked out of the conference that day with a new confidence and boldness. The faith she grew up believing was not only real to her experience but intellectually credible and even historically defensible. Rather than feeling inferior in class, she took every opportunity to share the reasons she had learned that Jesus is alive and Christianity is true. Today, Erica serves as a dedicated small group leader for senior high girls. Apologetics is one of her most helpful leadership tools as she answers her student's seemingly endless questions.

Erica's story reminded me of how a little information can shape minds and change lives. Christianity claims to be a truth that can set people free (John 8:32). Erica is one example of this. I want to see more stories like hers emerge during my lifetime. This little book could be a big help for some.

HOW CLEAR THINKING LEADS TO RIGHT LIVING

Erica showed me that when people get their doubts and questions about God sorted out, their once cloudy thinking becomes clear again. When people start thinking rightly about God, they start living rightly for him. The Bible has a lot to say to support how important our thinking is.

Whatever is true, whatever is honourable, whatever is just, whatever is pure, whatever is lovely, whatever is commendable, if there is any excellence, if there is anything worthy of praise, think about these things (Phil. 4:8).

We destroy arguments and every lofty opinion raised against the knowledge of God, and take every thought captive to obey Christ (2 Cor. 10:5).

What you think about really matters. It affects how you see the world, how you interact with the people in it, how you perceive yourself and most importantly what you believe about God. What you think about will affect how you live each day.

I wanted to write a book of Christian philosophy that could be read by people who were not philosophers. Most of us do not speak in syllogisms. We make logical fallacies simply going to the grocery store never mind while having a philosophical discussion. Most of us find we have all these questions and are wondering if anyone can help us find the truth. That's what I have tried to do here. Let me tell you how clear minds make dirty feet.

ABOUT THE TITLE

"Clear Minds & Dirty Feet" came after reflecting on a verse that comes from the Old Testament book of Isaiah. There was a role in biblical times known as "The Messenger." The messenger was a young person assigned to accompany a battalion in war. If a victory was won, the messenger would run home and report the news (see 2 Samuel 18:24-27). Since many battles were held far away from the city, long distances would have to be spanned across arid, sloped and rugged terrain. A messenger's feet, at the end of each journey would have been dirty, cracked and probably quite bloody. This, as it turns out, is a lovely sight in God's eyes. He says to Isaiah,

> How beautiful upon the mountains are the feet of him
> who brings good news, who publishes peace, who brings
> good news of happiness, who publishes salvation, who
> says to Zion, "Your God reigns" (Is. 52:7).

An excited messenger would have been a welcome sight for anyone who spotted him coming. Though the messenger's feet may not have been pretty to look at, they were most certainly beautiful to the one receiving the message. I read that passage and realized that I have my own experiences with dirty feet.

One of my greatest joys in life is speaking at youth summer camps. Every summer I see hundreds of campers commit their lives to Jesus. Eternity is altered every week at camp. It is the most exhilarating experience to be a part of this. I am simply a messenger of who God is and what he has done for people. Walking around camp barefoot or in flip-flops, my feet become filthy. They crack, they bleed, and the black/brown colour on the bottom would make any aesthetician cringe. These are the feet that only God could love.

It is my hope that you too will embrace the role of a messenger. You already are a messenger about many things. I'm sure you love talking about your favourite movies, celebrities, your sports team or some current event that has caught your attention. People naturally love sharing things that are important to them. I want you to start seeing why Christianity is worth getting your feet dirty telling others about.

With a title like this, clearly, I am concerned about the state of your mind and feet. As you learn these truths, the next step is to experience the thrill of getting your own feet dirty by sharing the truth with others.

To accomplish this I have written a book on Christian apologetics. It is for followers of Jesus and those who are checking Christianity out, investigating what Christians believe. Apologetics is the task of helping people see that the claims of

Christianity are not make-believe myths but actually true and very reasonable to accept. The verse that inspires such a task is found in 1 Peter 3:15:

> But in your hearts honor Christ the Lord as holy, always being prepared to make a defense to anyone who asks you for a reason for the hope that is in you; yet do it with gentleness and respect.

Peter commands Christians to always be ready to "give a reason" for the hope they have in Christ. This Greek word for defense is, *apologia*, hence the word, "apologetics." An apologia is still used in the Greek language today. It gives the picture of one standing before a court and defending a claim. Christians make claims like "God exists," "Jesus is alive", "The Bible comes from God" and many others. We must be able to defend these claims.

There are two kinds of people who will benefit from this book:

1. The Thinker Considering Believing

American satirist Mark Twain once called faith, "believing in something you know is not true." This is, sadly, the perception that many skeptics hold about Christianity. I want those who are curious to see that faith is not about believing in something despite all the evidence to the contrary. In fact, as we will see, the Christian faith works quite the opposite. Faith is looking at all the evidence for something and then making a decision based on what is most reasonable. Faith is looking at a chair and reasoning, "Now I know that chairs usually support me when I sit on them. This chair looks stable like the other chairs I have seen before. Therefore, I will put my faith in this chair and sit down." And then you put your faith in action and sit on it.

People who are checking out the Christian faith or are looking to disprove it are never told to "just believe" in it. Everyone is welcomed to question things with a critical mind. You are allowed to be a Christian and still hold on to your brain. You are going to need it. Observe how readers of the Old Testament prophet, Isaiah, are invited to engage their minds and explore the evidence for his writing. "Come now let us reason together"(Is. 1:18). God himself is the one doing the welcoming here. Even the gospel of John was written with the explicit objective to engage those who were curious about who Jesus is.

> Now Jesus did many other signs in the presence of the disciples, which are not written in this book; *but these are written so that you may believe that Jesus is the Christ, the Son of God,* and that by believing you may have life in his name (John 20:30-31).

If at any time during your reading of this book you think, "I think this is true. I would like to have this life that is offered," you can turn to the appendix at the end of the book. There are some instructions there that will help you work through the next steps.

2. The Believer Considering Thinking

Since I grew up in a hockey family, hockey was a huge part of what I remember as a kid. My brother and I played hockey on ice and on the street. After dinner, we finished the day by watching hockey. Our family team was always the Vancouver Canucks. My dad bought us jerseys which we proudly wore. As I got older, my enthusiasm for the Canucks waned. My teenage rebellion not only sought independence from my family, I even reconsidered whether I would be a Canucks fan at all. Thankfully, my dad never forced his team on me. He just kept cheering for Vancouver. Though, I could have picked any team, I landed on the Vancouver Canucks once again. Today, by my own personal choice, I am a long-suffering Vancouver Canucks fan.

Like my family and our Vancouver Canuck heritage, if you have been raised in the church, you know what it feels like to believe something simply because that's what your parents taught you.

Eventually, as you cut the apron strings from home, you start to explore your own beliefs. This is a perfectly natural part of becoming an adult. You do not want to just believe something because someone else told you. You want to believe something *because you know it is actually true.* Part of believing something is having good reasons, or evidence to believe it.

This book is for you because it will provide you with the reasons for why your Christian faith is intellectually credible. As a follower of Jesus, it is time to take your discipleship journey to the next level. It is time to learn what it means to "love God with all your mind" (Matt. 22:37). It is time to get your mind clear about what you believe about Jesus and why you believe it. The late C.S. Lewis, a popular Christian author, and Oxford University don, encourages us not to neglect this important part of Christian discipleship:

> God is no fonder of intellectual slackers than of any other slackers. If you are thinking of becoming a Christian, I warn you, you are embarking on something which is going to take the whole of you, brains and all. But, fortunately, it works the other way round. Anyone who is honestly trying to be a Christian will soon find his intelligence being sharpened: one of the reasons why it needs no special education to be a Christian is that Christianity is an education itself.[1]

This book is an invitation for you to rediscover the reasons for the hope with which you have been raised. My hope is that the skeptic and believer alike will encounter the truth. This truth, if properly applied will change how you live. It did with me. It did with Erica. It could with you as well.

This is how clear minds make dirty feet.

---

[1] C.S. Lewis. *Mere Christianity* (New York, NY: HarperCollins, 1952). p78.

EXAMINING YOUR WORLDVIEW:
WHAT TO BUILD A LIFE UPON

"Everyone then who hears these words of mine and does them will be like a wise man who built his house on the rock. And the rain fell, and the floods came, and the winds blew and beat on that house, but it did not fall, because it had been founded on the rock."

-Jesus, Matthew 7:24-25

On April 20, 2011, following a tsunami that killed tens of thousands of Japanese people, The *New York Times* published an article titled, "Tsunami Warnings: Written In Stone"[2] Along the coast of Japan, stone tablets were erected atop hillsides that call out to all who would heed its warning, "Do not build anything below here!"

Reporter Martin Fackler said that those who kept their villages above the line of the ancient stones were spared from the

---

[2] Martin Fackler. "Tsunami Warnings: Written In Stone" *The New York Times*. April 20, 2011.

tsunami. The waves stopped 300 feet below the warning stone. Previous generations, as far as six hundreds years before, knew about the destruction of tsunamis and warned following generations about its dangers. The problem is, not everyone listened. Following the boom years of post-World War II Japan, many communities were built along the coastline for cost and convenience sake. "As time passes, people inevitably forget, until another tsunami comes that kills 10,000 more people," lamented Fumio Yamashita. Modern day Japan forgot the warnings of the past, or perhaps they ignored them altogether. Either way, those who found themselves below the line were overtaken by the giant wave that tragically killed so many thousands that day.

This story is a warning for us all. The quote at the outset of this chapter is from Matthew 7. Jesus told a story of two kinds of foundations upon which two men had built houses. One house was built on a foundation of rock and the other upon sand. The house on rock was stable in a storm because of the strength of the foundation on which it stood. The other, because it had no strong foundation, was completely destroyed. Imagine if you saw this story on the news. A hurricane passed, and one house was left in ruins while the other stood strong. What would the owners say to the camera? How did they prepare for the storms? Did they even prepare at all?

I cannot help but think of those storm warning stones as I begin this book. If there ever were a time to consider the foundation upon which you are building your life on, now is that time. I have been referring to foundations, but I think a better word is *worldview*. Let's now consider the worldview on which you are building your life.

WHAT IS A WORLDVIEW?

Everyone has a worldview. Your worldview is what you believe to be most true about the world. A worldview answers the truly important questions of life. James Sire describes a worldview as:

...a commitment, a fundamental orientation of the heart, that can be expressed as a story or in a set of presuppositions (assumptions, that may be true, partially true, or false) which we hold (consciously or subconsciously) about the basic constitution of reality, and that provides that foundation on which we live and move and have our being.[3]

Sire's book, *The Universe Next Door,* is a highly used resource on the topic of worldview. Sire lists these eight questions that every worldview must answer:

- What is the prime or ultimate reality?
- Where did everything come from?
- What is a human being?
- What happens to a person after death?
- How do we really know what we know?
- How can we know the difference between right and wrong?
- What is the meaning of human history?
- What personal, life-orienting commitments are consistent with my worldview?

How you answer all these questions will determine what you live for and what is most important in life. Christianity answers all these questions in a way that is reasonable to the brain, satisfying to the heart and makes sense of our experience. C.S. Lewis explained it this way, "I believe in Christianity as I believe that the sun has risen – not only because I see it, but because by it, I see everything else."[4] For Lewis, Christianity helped him make sense of the world. It gave categories for why things

---

[3] James Sire. *The Universe Next Door: A Basic Worldview Course* (Downers Grove, ILL: InterVarsity Press, 2009).

[4] C.S. Lewis, "Is Theology Poetry?", in *Essay Collection and Other Short Pieces.* (London, Eng.: HarperCollins, 2000). p21.

happened, what the source of our problems was and what the solution would be. C.S. Lewis found the Christian worldview so compelling, he dropped his atheism and became a Christian.

Think about your own worldview for a moment. Have you taken the time to consider what you believe about the world? How do you form *your* strongest beliefs? What contributed to your shaping of these core convictions? Is there any room for God's involvement in the way you see the world?

Like I said, many people do not usually take the time to think about the foundation upon which they are building their lives. When it comes to buying a house, I see that people care a great deal about the foundations of the property they are about to buy. My dad is a realtor, and before he sells a house, before people trust him with the investment of hundreds of thousands of their dollars, he recommends the buyers hire a home inspector to carefully check the structural soundness of the house, and most importantly, the foundation upon which the potential investment is built. My dad would tell you that, no matter how beautiful or decorated it may be, without a strong foundation; it is doomed. If the foundation is cracked or unstable in any way, the house needs to be torn down and rebuilt on a proper base.

If this is how much we care about the foundation of our property, how much should we care about the foundation of *our lives*? I think most people are too busy working in their lives to look at what they are building their lives *on*. Rather than take the time to check, we just keep building.

In Jesus' parable about the two houses and the storm, one man refused to do the hard work of getting to the foundations of what he believed. He might have been content just doing whatever his friends, family members, or culture wanted him to do. Maybe work, sports or friends were calling louder than that small voice urging him to consider what his beliefs were. Sadly, when calamity came, he was shaken to the core and found out the hard way that there was no stability to his life at all.

The vast majority of this book is devoted to helping my readers understand the Christian worldview and why it is so important to see the world this way. If the Christian worldview is true, that means that any other worldview is a faulty foundation up which to build your house-life. If this is the case, take a lesson from the Japanese tsunami and abandon it immediately.

STORMS OF CHANGE

Beginning in the seventeenth century and following, a storm of intellectualism blew through Europe that sought to push Western Europe off its Christian worldview foundation and towards a secular approach. The Enlightenment brought many tremendous advances in medicine, education, government, and even reforms in the church. The Enlightenment rationalized another worldview upon which people could build their house. Atheism became an acceptable view about the truth of the universe. Atheism became more popular as the West slowly secularized. This movement away from God would not be without its consequences. No one saw this better than the prophet of the Enlightenment, a German philosopher named Friedrich Nietzsche.

THE DESPAIR OF NIHILISM

Friedrich Nietzsche (1844-1900) understood that a widespread embrace of atheism would be a big problem for society. Nietzsche, no fan of God or Christianity, knew that building a society on a Godless foundation would have enormous consequences for everyday life. Nietzsche foresaw the day when people would realize that the denial of God would usher in an age of true despair and hopelessness. He called it *nihilism*. Nihilism is a worldview that highlights the dire implications of a world without God. It argues that life is without objective meaning, purpose, or any kind of value because there is no God.

How could Nietzsche make these claims? Christian apologist, Dr. William Lane Craig, explains the origin of Nietzsche's dreary conclusions:

> Without God, the universe is the result of a cosmic accident, a chance explosion. There is no reason for which it exists. As for man, he's a freak of nature—a blind product of matter *plus* time *plus* chance. If God does not exist, then you are just a miscarriage of nature, thrust into a purposeless universe to live a purposeless life…the end of everything is death…In short, life is utterly without reason…Unfortunately, most people don't realize this fact. They continue on as though nothing has changed.[5]

Talking about foundations, the atheist worldview has little to build on, other than being a result of a cosmic accident that happened billions of years ago. With such an aimless beginning, there is no reason for the universe's existence and no particular destination in mind.

The nihilist looks around at everything and comes to terms with what seems to be obvious. The sun is one tiny dying star in an enormous universe. One day the sun will burn out or explode, destroying us all. The earth is a molten rock that could either be blown up by nuclear weapons or an erratic comet. We are one of the seven billion nameless faceless ones currently living on this rock. What does our existence matter to this rock floating around a dying star within the expanse of an enormous universe?

Not much.

This rock has seen billions of years of living organisms and will see many more once we die and turn to dirt. Our life is but one tiny, brief, insignificant piece of this vast universe. So, why, the nihilist argues, do people really think that it is important to be a

---

[5] William Lane Craig. *On Guard: Defending Your Faith with Reason and Precision* (Colorado Springs: David C. Cook, 2010), p37.

"good person", get good grades, or get a good job? What difference could that possibly make to anything?

Nihilism is an honest evaluation of what a universe without God would look like. Nietzsche was right about that. Where he went wrong was in thinking this was true of the actual universe.

Nietzsche wrote a famous short story titled, *The Madman*. This story highlights the implications of what a society without God would imply. In Nietzsche's story a madman runs through a town crying out to the townspeople,

> Whither is God? I shall tell you. We have killed him - you and I. All of us are his murderers ... God is dead... And we have killed him. How shall we, the murderers of all murderers, comfort ourselves?[6]

Nietzsche's question is a very good one: *How do we comfort ourselves in a world without God?* How do people cope without God?

In the spring of 2012, I caught a glimpse of how modern people answered this question. I visited an English university as part of a team conducting a worldview survey with the students there. Our goal was to survey these students and help them sort out what core beliefs lay at the foundation of their lives. Many of the students I talked to denied the existence of God. Understandably, this was a secular, liberal English institution. While doing the survey I noticed that when it came to living out the implications of their commitment to a world without God, they rejected Nietzsche's conclusions. These students *did not like* the idea that, without God, life was without meaning, purpose or value. Many said that they felt they had a great deal of meaning in their relationships, their goals and in their studies.

---

[6] Friedrich Nietzsche. *The Gay Science* . Walter Kaufmann ed. (New York: Vintage, 1974), pp.181-182

Are you a nihilist? Where do you find meaning, purpose and value in your life here on earth? Is there any? I would suspect, that, like the students I surveyed in England, you do want to feel like your life matters, and that is why there is an alternative worldview. Rather than focus on the bleak conclusions of nihilism, the students preferred a more happy alternative - the worldview of existentialism.

CAN WE MAKE LIFE MEANINGFUL?

When philosophers talk about secular existentialism, they often mention one of the leading thinkers in this movement, Albert Camus (1913-1960).[7] In his book, *The Myth of Sisyphus* this French philosopher and author searched for meaning in light of life's supposed meaninglessness. In the last chapter of this famous essay, Camus built on an old Greek mythological character- Sisyphus. Sisyphus was famous for getting caught cheating Hades, the god of death. For this he was punished by Zeus, sentenced to push a heavy stone up a hill all day. Once he reached the top of the hill, the stone rolled back down to the bottom. He was forced to do this every day, forever. Camus relates this experience to the factory workers of his day and compares Sisyphus' fate to the meaninglessness of boring, purposeless factory work which was consuming their lives.

Camus writes, "The workman of today works every day in his life at the same tasks, and this fate is no less absurd [than that of Sisyphus]. But it is tragic only at the rare moments when it becomes conscious."[8] Here Camus observes that life is meaningless, but as long as people are distracted enough by work and other pursuits, they will thankfully never realize it. In light of life's meaninglessness, Sisyphus wonders what the

---

[7] Kierkegaard's Christian existentialism is a whole other can of worms that will not be covered in this book.

[8] Albert Camus. *The Myth of Sisyphus*. (London, Eng. Vintage Books, 1991).

appropriate response should be for those who figure it out. Camus declares, "There is but one truly serious philosophical problem, and that is suicide. Judging whether life is or is not worth living amounts to answering that fundamental question of philosophy."[9]

The Myth of Sisyphus makes us wonder if we too are like the ones who are so distracted making friends with important people, staying on top of the latest technology, getting good marks in school, and making lots of money, that we never pause to think:

What are we *actually* living for?

Sisyphus ended up opening his heart to questions of meaning, value and purpose. He himself decided it was best to just make the most of his short time on earth, however meaningless it all may be. Through Sisyphus, Camus is telling us that life is a joke, and the courageous ones will accept that and have a laugh along the way. I know many movies released these days that operate under the same premise.

This is the mantra of existentialism: *make the most of our days in light of life's meaninglessness.* To an existentialist, you have the responsibility of putting whatever meaning you want into your life.

If you want your story to be about money, you can make it about money. If family is what matters most to you, make your life about family. If you want your life to be about maximizing the experience of life's pleasures - who can stop you from doing your best to have the most pleasure you possibly can?

This approach has worked for some people. They are doing their own thing: going to work, raising a family, living in the suburbs, peacefully cutting their grass on weekends, and being good

---

[9] Camus, p3.

citizens. No God, church or organized religion is getting in the way of what they want to do with their lives.

The problem with this kind of thinking is that one cannot just go about assigning meaning and worth to something as if *they* were the sole arbiter and authority of it. What if someone felt that the environment had no value. Would it still be worth preserving? What if they thought that poor people were worthless? What if everyone thought the poor were worthless? Would these human beings still hold any worth in society? The problem with existentialism is that it is too individualistic and subjective. The dignity of people, the meaning of human life and the value of things should not be individually determined. We humans are too selfish, narrow-minded and finite to be making such judgments.

Another reason existentialism fails as a worldview is because life is really terrible for some people. They cannot get meaning from things because they have nothing. They cannot make their life about making money because they have no money. It cannot be about family because the family they grew up in was terrible, broken or abusive. Perhaps they have really wanted to start a family of their own and, for various reasons, they have not been able to do so. Perhaps they have failed at personal relationships and find themselves very lonely. Some people can no longer fool themselves into thinking the purpose of their existence is to achieve the success they were taught was theirs to have. They were not smart enough, pretty enough, or rich enough to become the picture of success of which they had aimed. Life experience has forced these people to shift their worldview from being existentialists to nihilists. They have given up thinking their life has any meaning at all and now, heartbroken, they conclude that it is no use even trying anymore.

In September 2012, *Macleans* magazine wrote a startling article called "Campus Crisis: The Broken Generation." The tag line for the article was "Why so many of our best and brightest students report feeling hopeless, depressed, even suicidal." The article examined the dire condition of student mental health on university campuses today. Toronto's Ryerson University experienced a two hundred per cent increase in crisis situations at their counselling centre. In 2011, 1600 University of Alberta students were polled and over half of the students confessed that they had "felt things were hopeless." Another half said they had struggled with "overwhelming anxiety" in the past year. A shocking seven percent said that in the past year they had "seriously considered" committing suicide. Observed one counsellor of the problems over at Western University, "The past few years, it's [the need for crisis counselling] been growing exponentially." The problem spans across North America. After a string of student suicides, Cornell University in New York had to build nets around the seven bridges around campus to prevent students from jumping.

It seems that rather than abandon their worldview, many young people are abandoning their lives altogether. I am disturbed to see the number of suicides and suicide attempts by those between the ages of fourteen and twenty-five. Many of their suicide notes report they had lost meaning, purpose and a sense that life held any value.

This is no longer just about philosophy. This is about the very real lives we are all trying to make sense of here on Earth.

THE HOPEFUL ALTERNATIVE

Jesus gave us hope that there could be more to life than what the West is currently experiencing. Jesus said directly, "I have come that they may have life and have it in full..." (John 10:10). Given the options of the hopelessness of nihilism or the shallow pursuits of existentialism, it is nice to know there is another alternative. This is the difference that Jesus makes.

When considering the topic of spirituality or religion, I would encourage you to look at Christianity first. It is a testable religion. That is, it is based on evidence. The evidence is philosophical and historical. It can be examined and then we can all make our decision.

What follows in this book are the evidences that will satisfy our mind's search for truth, our heart's desire for love, and our soul's aching for meaning and purpose. These are the truths that have inspired and continue to inspire people with a sense of purpose for their future, meaning in their present day, and redemption for their past. How can such a worldview provide this?

The Apostle Peter told Christians to always be ready to give reasons for the hope they profess. I would like to share mine with you now. The following chapters are my evidences for the hope that I have found in Jesus. These are my reasons why you can believe Christianity is true and a worthy foundation upon which to build *your* life.

FAITH AND SCIENCE:
WHAT ALL THE FUSS IS ABOUT

"I was assuming that the human mind is completely ruled by reason. But that is not so...the battle is between faith and reason on one side and emotion and imagination on the other."

-C.S. Lewis

It is popular these days to argue that the study of science is incompatible with any sort of religious belief. Both Christians and non-Christians alike seem to think that you have to choose between the Christian faith or modern science. Since this is a widely held belief both inside and outside the church, there are people on both sides who hold it. This chapter seeks to understand some of the motivations behind this position and why it is the wrong approach to take.

Often, when I ask a skeptic why they don't believe in God, many will respond with the very unfortunate line:

"I don't believe in God. I believe in science."

That answer saddens me. When you take the time to look at the real relationship between faith and science, you find the two are not enemies; rather, they are friends. Granted, they are friends that do not always agree on everything. No friendship ever does. They have their points of tension. Every friendship has these as well. As friends, faith and science have a great deal of history together. They work hard to hold each other accountable and challenge one another to be better (I hope you have friends like that too).

What if, after all, you did not have to choose between believing in God and being committed to the findings of science?

In this chapter I will unravel some popularly held misconceptions and show where the true tension in this friendship really lies. To remain somewhat concise, I have had to ignore or omit an embarrassingly large amount of material that would have been helpful. However, the points I will try to cover should give you enough to get a start along a path that will help you understand the discussion a bit better.

Let me highlight five things you need to know about the relationship between the Christian faith and science:

1. SCIENCE CAN NEITHER PROVE NOR DISPROVE THE EXISTENCE OF GOD

The claim that science can disprove God's existence is an honest ambition but it is a statement that is actually impossible to back up. This is because the task of proving something like science is unprovable by scientific methods. How do you prove an idea like "science"? What container do you use to measure it? What laws of science do you use to prove science? That's the first reason why the worldview of *scientism*, the belief that science proves everything, fails to work out in real life. Science cannot prove everything because it cannot even prove itself.

You need something more than just the scientific method to explain the world in which we live. Beware of false dichotomies (either/or situations) that proponents of scientism assume. You should never have to choose whether or not you believe in either a plane's engine or gravity. You can have both. You shouldn't have to accept the existence of Steve Jobs or the iPhone; nor should you have to decide whether you believe in God or science. Those who insist that scientific discoveries disprove God are mistaken.

While studying at the *University of Oxford*, I found myself dialoguing with some brilliant students who were studying in various scientific fields. Most of these students held a healthy respect for various academic disciplines outside of their own scientific field. They reported spending most of their days looking at numbers, planets, chemicals, brain synapses, bacteria cultures, etc. The role of the scientist is to say, "On this day, under these conditions with these variables, this is what I observed..." Just because they were "scientists" did not mean that they were consumed with talking about the naturalistic origins of the universe all day.

This is because science is about things that happen in the *physical* world. It deals with physical matter and how it operates. Science explores causes and effects. The rest of life: things like love, politics, art, relationships, or God is up to the humanities to figure out. I was pleased to note that many Oxford scientists sat beside me each week at the always student-friendly, *Saint Ebbes Anglican Church*. These friends of mine who work in the scientific world all day obviously saw no conflict between their Christian beliefs and their work as scientists.

Perhaps no contemporary Christian with a world class scientific credential has better described the harmony of faith and science than John Polkinghorne. Polkinghorne enjoyed success as a mathematical physicist at the *University of Cambridge* before becoming an Anglican theologian. In, *Theology in the Context of Science*, he writes how studying our "rationally transparent" universe is "beautiful, rewarding scientists with the experience of wonder at the marvellous order which is revealed through the labours of their research." Polkinghorne expresses that his scientific study does not disprove God. Rather, he is rewarded for working hard as a scientist with gaining a higher appreciation for God.[10]

Not all would agree with Polkinghorne or my scientist friends at Oxford. Consider this claim by renowned Oxford scientist, Peter Atkins, "Humanity should accept that science has eliminated the justification for believing in cosmic purpose and that any survival of purpose is inspired only by sentiment."[11]

Perhaps you or someone you know is a firm believer that the cumulative effort of scientific discovery has successfully eliminated God and our need to ever talk about him again.

This belief, that science eradicates (the need for) God, is a myth many people believe today. The truth is that science, the study of the world and collection of our findings, has not and cannot disprove God. There is no scientific journal that has disproven God's existence. This is because God cannot be put in a test tube and either verified or falsified. God is a spiritual being and is outside the reach of empirical scientific research. Christians cannot prove God the existence of God with absolute certainty, nor can atheists disprove his existence with any certainty. That does not mean that we cannot look at the evidence as to whether or not God exists. We will do this in the following chapters. There I will show why there is an overwhelming amount of

---

[10] John Polkinghorne. *Theology in the Context of Science.* (Yale University, 2009.) p90.

[11] Peter Atkins, "Will Science Ever Fail?" *New Scientist*, August 8,1992, p32-35.

evidence to believe that God *does* exist. For now, I just want to state that science can not prove or disprove the existence of God. As we will now see, there are many other areas into which science simply cannot reach.

2. THE THINGS THAT MATTERS MOST IN LIFE ARE UNSCIENTIFIC

Biologist Sir Peter Medawar confesses some limitations to what pure science can discuss. When we think about it, these limitations are pretty important. Medawar writes:

> The existence of a limit to science is made clear by its inability to answer childlike, elementary questions having to do with first and last things: "How did everything begin?' 'What is the point of living?" "What are we here for?"[12]

Those are three big questions to which we all want answers. They are the kinds of questions that keep people up at night. According to Medawar, we need more than the beaker and bunsen burner can offer us. These tools of science are unable to help us answer this kind of big existential questions.

To illustrate this limitation, consider the flower. Whatever the scientific world tells you about the DNA of flowers, it cannot explain why men give them to their mothers, girlfriends or wives to show them love (or to ask forgiveness). It seems a little counter-intuitive when you think about it. The giving of flowers is the handing off of a dying plant. A person receives it with a smile, puts it in water, and for the next week watches it slowly deteriorate and die. How this demonstrates love is one of the great mysteries of humankind. I once heard comedian Demetri Martin suggest that this process should be what we do to

---

[12] As quoted in John Lennox's, *God and Stephen Hawking*, Kindle Locations p168-171

threaten someone. We should hand our enemies a dozen daisies and say: "Watch this...this will happen to you."

Of course, this will never happen. Flowers are too cute to be considered a threat. Any smart man knows that flowers are a time tested method to win a woman's heart over (or win it over again after you've done something stupid). The pure science of a flower alone cannot explain the power of a flower. You cannot reduce flowers to reproducing angiosperms or their elements of carbon, oxygen, hydrogen, calcium and phosphorus in order to understand why people love them so much. Trying to scientifically explain the phenomenon of flower-giving is a waste of time. That is why if you spend too much time in a lab coat, you will struggle to find a girlfriend. My point is simply that the use of science alone as an explanatory force has its limitations.

If you don't prefer illustrations about flowers, this sports analogy should suffice instead. The study of science is like understanding the rules of a sport like basketball, for example. The rules tell you the boundaries of play, the rules that govern the players and of what material the ball is made. The rules cannot, however, tell you about why people play basketball, nor can they measure the competition, the passion, the joy or the camaraderie of team dynamics. To further the analogy, we should never have to choose between *how* we play basketball and *why* we play basketball. They can and should work together.

Science cannot explain love, beauty, music, poetry, heartbreak, friendship, justice, romance, or how to have a relationship with God. These are, ironically enough, the things people feel are what matter *most* in life. If you want to study these things, you need to leave the boundaries within which material science operates.

My old professor, Dr. John Lennox, once told a story illustrating the limits of science and how it needs help to make sense of things. I thought a few pictures would help flesh the story out a bit.

THE CAKE STORY WITH THE MANY LAYERS

Every year there was a gathering of secular naturalists.

Since many of Matilda's friends were there, she wanted to help them celebrate. She made them a cake.

Matilda worked hard in the kitchen all day preparing the best cake she had ever made.

She walked across town with the cake and dropped it off where the naturalists were gathering.

"Hey, everyone!" said one attendee. "There's a cake at the door!"

The attendees were very excited to have such a lovely cake at the party.

One man took a look at it and explained all that he saw before him.

"This cake consists of flour, eggs, sugar and baking powder and a layer of red icing. What more could possibly be said about it?" he asked.

"There is more to add," quipped another. "These ingredients are made up of much smaller elements: hydrogen, carbon, iron, oxygen, calcium, phosphorus, sulfur, sodium, and magnesium."

"That's not all," added another. "My research tells me that those elements are a combination of conjoined molecules which are made up of even smaller atoms and even smaller quarks. Not much more can be known about this cake."

A fourth fellow stepped into the circle. Taking a big swipe of icing with his finger he added, "And when the icing touches your tongue, it sends a signal to your brain which tells you that it is indeed very sweet to taste. The cake is quite tasty."

All four sat there smugly thinking they had explained everything that there was to know about the cake. That's when one inquisitive voice came from behind them,

"Does anyone know how this cake came got here?"

The crowd murmured a few ideas, but no one was taking responsibility for the tasty dessert. Who made the cake? The crowd was a little embarrassed. They were all so busy studying the cake that nobody asked about how it got there.

Matilda stepped into the circle and solved the mystery.

"My friends, today I made this cake," said Matilda very confidently. "And I made it so I could tell you that...well, that I love you and I thought a cake would be a good way to show it."

THE END

The people at the party proudly knew all the "whats" about Matilda's cake. They knew all about its contents, its chemistry and the reason for its sweet flavour. What they did not know is where it came from and why it was brought to the party. This story serves as a fitting example of both the joys and limits of science. Science will fascinate us by highlighting the wonder of the universe we live in. Theology will tell us why our universe is there in the first place and what purpose it serves.

I once had a conversation with an Oxford student whose undergraduate work focused on virtual reality. An expert in neurology, he was also a determinist. Determinists argue that *all* our lives are already predetermined by physics and can be detected by studying our brain waves. To him, a human being is little more than the result of predetermined synapses in the brain playing out their course.

I felt sad for this bright chap because I could tell he actually believed this. He did not see that there was much more to life beyond his area of scientific expertise.

You cannot describe a human being by physics alone. Other scientific disciplines must be considered as well. The chemist can break a human body down into chemicals and sell them for about five dollars at a local hardware store. Biologists can reduce you to cells and DNA. Sociologists would add their expertise, saying you are also a product of your family, culture and various other relationships you have developed in your life. The theologian has a very important voice to add to this conversation as well. The theologian would read the Bible and deduce that you are more than your brain waves, your DNA, your chemicals, your culture or your family - you were made by God and for God. As your creator, he loves you, wants a relationship with you and has a plan for your life. This reveals why it is important to have a number of disciplines at the table and not just one. The sciences gives us the what and how about what makes up a human being. Most importantly, I believe, theology gives us the who and why behind what makes us human. They should all work together.

When it comes to the relationship between faith and science, we must remember that scientists themselves are only human.

3. STATEMENTS BY SCIENTISTS ARE NOT ALWAYS SCIENTIFIC STATEMENTS

This syllogism helps us see why not everything that is said by someone in a lab coat is absolute truth.

Premise one: All scientists are human beings.
Premise two: Human beings sometimes make errors.
Conclusion: Therefore, sometimes scientists make errors.

Disagreement amongst scientists in all fields of science are common. Since nobody has access to all knowable truth, scientific research is always challenging accepted theory in order to advance knowledge.

When two scientists do not agree about something, they do not throw up their hands and say, "Well, you believe what you want, and I will believe what I want." Instead, they wrestle it out, and the winner usually ends up winning a Nobel Prize.

Sometimes, disagreements among scientists are the result of interpretation, not based on observable data, but as a result of the biases and worldview of the scientists making the interpretation. Consider the current climate change debate. Both sides of the argument are extremely skeptical about the driving presuppositions behind the other's conclusions.

It takes practice to spot a worldview within a statement. If you are looking, you can find these hidden philosophical interpretations all the time. For example, when a textbook refers to an adaptation of one species to another species, it will often be referred to as a "blind" or "random" process. Within these carefully chosen words there is a hidden premise that there is nothing guiding these observed adaptations; nor is there any goal towards which these changes are headed. It is all just a process of "random blindness."

If writers of textbooks believe there is nothing guiding history, they believe the world is *ateleological* (without a goal). Try to catch how physicist, Dr. Andrei Linde, reveals his ateleological worldview as he describes how our universe came to support life. He writes, "We have a lot of really, really strange coincidences, and all of these coincidences are such that they make life possible."[13] The clue is in the word "coincidences". How does Linde know these adaptations are coincidences? It is because his worldview demands that *since there is no God* there can only be coincidences. According to his worldview, there can be no ultimate purpose for anything. There is no goal to evolution. It just happens. That is why any mutation, advantageous or not, is always a coincidence.

If, however, you believe in a God who not only exists but has been and is guiding the course of the world, you will have a *teleological* interpretation of history. "Teleological" comes from the Greek word, "telos" meaning, "end." God made everything with a plan and an end in mind. If you believe God is involved with the world like this, that will determine how you interpret the observable data and how you explain it to others.

The only way to absolutely know what happens behind the scenes of these adaptations (and all other world events for that matter) is to step outside of science and into the realm of metaphysics. If there is no God, then, yes, everything is random, blind and purposeless. All life on earth merely stumbles along towards no particular end. On the other hand, if there is a God, there *is* a purpose because God is behind it all.

Before we move on, I want to give one more example of how worldview determines interpretation.

When Biologists Dabble in Philosophy

---

[13] Check out the article at: www.discovermagazine.com/2008/dec/10-sciences-alternative-to-an-intelligent-creator. Accessed February 10, 2013.

Of course, everyone is entitled to practise science and still contribute to other topics like philosophy, cultural anthropology , theology and all other fields of knowledge for that matter. They just need to be honest when they are making the jump from their area of expertise to another discipline. Watch how Richard Dawkins seamlessly hops from biology into philosophy in this popular quote regarding how he feels DNA relates to the meaning of life.

> The universe we observe has precisely the properties we should expect if there is, at bottom, no design, no purpose, no evil and no good, nothing but blind, pitiless indifference...DNA neither cares nor knows. DNA just is. And we dance to its music.[14]

Here Dawkins has made both an observation about DNA and then adds his interpretation of how it fits with his view of how the world runs (his worldview). The DNA part he gets from his expertise; biology. The other ("no design, no purpose, no evil, no good," etc.), he borrows from philosophy, anthropology and psychology. Science has shown Professor Dawkins that humans are made of DNA. DNA is a major contributor to what you are made of, and it will determine a significant portion of what your life will look like. It will tell you about your hair colour, your eyes, and whether or not you will struggle with high blood pressure. These are all determined by your DNA. But is that *all* that makes you who you are? According to Dawkins, yes, it is. That is now his interpretation of the data coming through- that you are DNA and *nothing but DNA*. He is concluding that there is no purpose to life but dancing to DNA. To him, there are no objective morals, there is no purpose and there is no God to give our lives a sense of purpose. Of course, one cannot determine all of this through a microscope or a test tube. These are

---

[14] Richard Dawkins. *The Blind Watchmaker (New York, NY: WW Norton, 1995)* p.133.

metaphysical, philosophical claims which Dawkins is happy to make and lump in with his biological findings.

There Is Always More Going On

One of the most prominent myths about science is that it is always neutral and objective. Thomas Nagel is an atheist who offers a helpful insight as he confesses how scientists come to their work, loaded with their own presuppositions. He writes in *The Last Word*,

> I want atheism to be true and am made uneasy by the fact that some of the most intelligent and well-informed people I know are religious believers. It isn't just that I don't believe in God, and, naturally, hope that I'm right about my belief - it's that I hope there is no God. I don't want there to be a God; I don't want the universe to be like that.[15]

My point here is to make you aware of something that can easily fly under the radar, if you are not aware of it. I want to help you see that rather than simply believing everything someone in a white lab coat says, we must always follow the evidence ourselves. We must engage in critical thinking, accepting our own biases and acknowledging how each person's worldview determines how scientific data is interpreted and then applied.

Like all human activities, science is driven by worldview. Those who do not want God will find reasons why he is not there. Those who are searching for God will find evidence for him as well. Do not be surprised when these motivations come out in the scientific community. You should even look for them. Though Nagel may not want God, he observes that there are many intelligent people he respects who find no conflict with God and science. This kind of honesty is refreshing and a good

---

[15] Thomas Nagel, *The Last Word*. (Oxford University Press, New York, NY, 1997).

reminder for us to be aware that not all statements made by scientists are scientific statements.

4. SMART PEOPLE ARE NOT ALWAYS ATHEISTS

I have read literature from atheists who are geniuses. Likewise, I have read literature from Christians of equal genius. Both write at the highest levels of academia. Both win academic awards. Many skeptics will have you think the smartest people in the world are either atheists or agnostics. They would have you think that belief in God is something that should preoccupy children, like the tooth fairy, Santa Claus or unicorns. The truth is, they are only partially correct.

There are many in the Christian family who publicly reject any kind of intellectualism and resort instead to what is called "obscurantism" (believing in something despite all the evidence to the contrary).

Does your family have a weird uncle? Do you want to be judged based on his behaviour? The behaviour of the weird uncles in the Christian family does harm to the Christian reputation but does little to disprove Christianity. Just as atheists do not want to be judged by the behaviour of Stalin or Hitler or Mao, they should return the favour and not think every Christian is like this minority of the human race. Doing this is to make the error of collectivism, mistakenly thinking the fringe represents the whole. As a Christian, I personally follow Jesus who was able to debate with academics of his time (scribes and Pharisees). I honour the intellectual legacy of his disciples like the Apostle Paul, St. Augustine, Aquinas, Pascal, Kepler, C.S. Lewis, Alvin Plantinga, William Lane Craig and many other brilliant men and women in church history.

What about today? Are the best scientists in the modern world all atheists? This is the fear of many uninformed Christians and an arrogant assumption put forward by some atheists. The misconception is that the smarter you get, the less you believe in

God. Sociologist Elaine Howard Eklund researched this idea and found it to be false. In 2010, she published her findings in a book called *Science vs. Religion: What Scientists Really Think*. From 2005-2008, Eklund randomly surveyed 1700 scientists from twenty-one elite US universities. She found that nearly fifty percent of them had strong religious convictions.[16] Additionally, for the irreligious fifty percent, it was not their science that led them to atheism. Their rejection of God was motivated by the same reasons that people from other professions reject the Christian faith. These reasons included: not being raised in a Christian home; having bad experiences with the church; or having moral objections to the God of the Bible.[17]

According to Eklund's research, the scientific community is split regarding spiritual matters. I could tell you a whole number of occupations that are just as divided when it comes to belief in God. For example, you will find the same divide with medical doctors, politicians, musicians, plumbers, businessmen and school teachers. This same divide runs between the rich and the poor, the young and the old. The true conflict lies in worldview, between those who believe in God and those who do not.

Within theism, there are many disagreement of which you might already be aware. None is more debated than the contentious topic of evolution and Genesis 1.

5. UNDERSTANDING GENESIS 1 AND EVOLUTION

I want to warn you about the path upon which we are about to tread. When it comes to discussing evolution, many Christians have spoken out of ignorance and ended up looking like fools in the process.

---

[16] Elaine Howard Eklund. *Science vs. Religion: What Scientists Really Think*. (Oxford, Eng. Oxford University Press, 2010).

[17] *Ibid.*

Our caution comes to us from an "old" pastor named Saint Augustine. Augustine, writing long ago in the fourth century, had bad experiences with some fellow Christians who spoke ignorantly and misrepresented the Bible. They turned many people away from Christianity. Conscious that many of us are doing this exact thing I include this lengthy quote:

> It is a disgraceful and dangerous thing...to hear a Christian, presumably giving the meaning of Holy Scripture, talking nonsense on these topics [science]...The shame is not so much that an ignorant individual is derided, but that people outside the household of faith think our sacred writers held such opinions... If they find a Christian mistaken in a field which they themselves know well and hear him maintaining his foolish opinions about our books, how are they going to believe those books in matters concerning the resurrection of the dead, the hope of eternal life, and the kingdom of heaven? ...to defend their utterly foolish and obviously untrue statements, they will try to call upon Holy Scripture for proof and even recite from memory many passages which they think support their position, although they understand neither what they say nor the things about which they make assertion.[18]

When I first read this quote, I had to sit back in my chair and have a long, quiet think. It was a sobering reminder for me to stay humble when wading into the controversial waters of Genesis 1 and its relationship to modern day science. For as long as 1600 years, those who have preceded us have made mistakes. I do not want to repeat them. I would rather learn from them.

I want to be careful not to allow scientists free reign to parade around as theologians, nor to permit theologians to arrogantly

---

[18] Augustine. "The Literal Meaning of Genesis." This translation is by J. H. Taylor in *Ancient Christian Writers*, (Newman Press, 1982), Volume 41.

step outside of their expertise and pretend to be scientists. I have seen both abuses.

Evolution is a controversial topic. It always has been since it was first introduced. Interestingly, the controversy has had Christians and non-Christians arguing on both sides. There have always been Christians who saw no problem embracing evolution and there are those who have absolutely opposed it. I want to look at where some of the tension lies in hopes of clearing up some of the confusion with such a loaded term like "evolution."

What Do You Mean by "Evolution"?

I am often asked, "Do you believe in evolution?" It's a tough question to answer. It depends on what you mean by "evolution." Evolution is not an alternative worldview trying to explain away God. That is a fitting description of atheism, but it is not evolution.

When talking about the biological mechanism of how organisms change (what is popularly called "evolution"), it is important to begin by specifying what kind of change is being referenced. Just how many types of evolution there are is a contestable issue. I want us to be aware of two for now, though there are as many as six that get thrown around. I want to look at *Microevolution* and *Macroevolution*. Microevolution is the process of change in which a beneficial mutation leads to the enhancement of a species. This simple cartoon will help illustrate how microevolution helps turn a couple of white rabbits living in the Arctic into a very successful, thriving bunch of happy rabbits.

WHY I BELIEVE IN MICROEVOLUTION

A black rabbit once lived in the Arctic. He lived peaceably with all his neighbours — except for the polar bears. They often ate his friends and family.

One day a hungry polar bear went looking throughout the snow-covered land for something or someone to eat.

He spotted the black rabbit from a long distance. The rabbit was, after all, quite easy to see.
The polar bear made short work of the black rabbit by eating him for lunch.

Nearby, there lived a white rabbit named Tommy. He usually just minded his own business and tried not to bother anyone. He mostly liked to blend in with his surroundings.

The polar bear got hungry again and went looking for something or someone to eat.
He got very close to Tommy.

Because Tommy had white fur, the polar bear did not see him. The polar bear just walked on by and continued to look for food.

One day Tommy found a nice looking girl rabbit who was also able to avoid the hungry bear because of her white fur. They eventually got married.

Tommy and his wife did what rabbits do best: they settled down and started up a nice family full of white-furred rabbits.

MICROEVOLUTION AND MACROEVOLUTION

Universally accepted, microevolution has limits for what it can explain. These limits do not reach the center where the controversy lies - the *Thesis of Common Ancestry* was popularized by Charles Darwin. Darwin believed that the world we see today has come to us through an evolutionary process called natural selection. Through genetic mutation, species adapt and develop because the strongest of a species will survive and pass on their DNA to their successors. Macroevolution is the belief that all development — from the first moments of the universe, the formation of stars and planets, to the eventual emergence of simple bacteria, to the most complex human being is explainable through this naturalistic transformational process.

Wherever you land on the micro or macro evolution scale, both are incomplete to explain our origins. They both need some sort of being (such as "God," as theists suggest) to explain how everything started. Many skeptics and Christians fail to see that natural selection itself cannot explain where life began. The process of natural selection is *fully dependent* upon the existence of an original host from which it can mutate and duplicate. Even Richard Dawkins admits this:

> We have no evidence about what the first step in making life was, but we do know the kind of step it must have been. It must have been whatever it took to get natural selection started...And that means the key step was the rising, by some process as yet unknown, of a self-replicating entity.[19]

The most important point to remember from reading Genesis 1 and 2 is that whatever happened back then - God did it.

---

[19] Richard Dawkins. *The Greatest Show On Earth.* (New York, NY: Free Press, 2009). See chapter 13.

How God did it is where people hold varying positions. [Note that this discussion, like the topic of Hell, is also nestled comfortably within the already assumed existence of God.] We have conceded that something or someone needed to start everything. What happened after "In the beginning God…"? This is a very interesting topic for discussion.

As I said earlier, there are dedicated Christian men and women who completely disagree with each other here. I know some Christians who hold PhDs in biology and believe humans share common ancestry with chimpanzees. Then again, there are other highly educated Christians who (for scientific and other reasons) object strongly to the theory of macroevolution. To them, the transitions from nothing to something, from non-living to living, from impersonal living matter to personal living beings, and from non-rational beings to rational ones, is too large a leap of faith without some kind of divine intervention.

The debate to discover more about how God made the world will carry on as scientific research advances. Further discoveries will show by what means God brought about life and all the intricate biological complexity that we observe in the world today. I have observed that people who believe in God and the authority of the Bible can believe in evolution as well. But, they must have good reasons for doing so and be able to defend their position as well.

The purpose of this chapter was to show how theology tells us that God is the God of the whole world and that science tells us how God made and sustains it. What I hope I have done is to take the issue of evolution off the table, so that it is no longer a hindrance to your believing in God. The good news is that, if you are a theist, you can simply follow the evidence wherever it leads. The controversial first chapters of Genesis leave room for various interpretations, including an evolutionary process guided by God himself.[20]

If you are an atheist, there is no other alternative but to believe in spontaneous random life passed on through the blind process of natural selection. The atheist's commitment to nothing but materialism keeps him adamant to never allow a "divine foot in the door."[21] Thus, I think theistic scientists are in a far better position to be open minded to all the possibilities of how the cosmos came to be the way it is today.

GOD DID IT, BUT DOES THAT REALLY SETTLE IT?

As someone who works with kids aged 8-88, I get asked a lot about angels, demons, and dinosaurs as well as how God made the world, then flooded it and all the interesting characters that show up in Genesis. Honestly, it would have been more helpful if Genesis shed more light on these tough questions. The first book of the Bible seems a lot less concerned about explaining matters of science and prehistoric activity than it does about teaching us what we need to know about God and how he relates with people. It does this by telling us the stories of Adam and Eve, Noah, Abraham, Isaac, Jacob and Joseph.

Given what we do know, I have met many sincere Christians who have provided me with all sorts of perspectives on how Genesis 1 and 2 should be interpreted. They often get very creative and it is always interesting to listen to them.

Some Christians who read about the six days of creation in Genesis 1 mix them with some Old Testament dates, add in some

---

[20] One of the best books that surveys these interpretations is John Lennox's *Seven Days That Divide The World* (Grand Rapids, Mich : Zondervan, 2011).

[21] Richard Lewontin. Review of Carl Sagan's *The Demon-Haunted World: Science as a Candle in the Dark* (The New York Review, January, 9 1997). p. 31

New Testament genealogies, do a little math and conclude that the world is less than ten thousand years old. Though it is curious to me how there could be twenty-four hour days prior to the creation of a sun *and* why God would make such a young earth appear so very old, this group is still convinced that the earth was made in *six literal days*.

I do not agree with this position because I think it tries to read Genesis like a modern day science text book and not like how its original audience would have read it. I also think that it does not line up with the findings of cosmology and various other approaches to dating the earth. That being said, I have heard the critiques of the "Young Earth Creationists" and know why they still hold the position that they do. Though I do not agree with them, I respect the reasons why my brothers and sisters do so.

Others, just as committed to proper Biblical interpretation as the young earth crew, come up with another way to read the creation account. The Day-Age view is a perspective whereby the days of Genesis 1 represent long periods (millions or even billions of years) of time. For example, some scholars think that the gap between verses 1:1 and 1:2, between the beginning of time and the beginning of God speaking, is an indeterminate amount of time.[22] Also, the Hebrew word for day, "yom," could be seen as a "beginning and an end" rather than a literal twenty-four hour period.

You should know that in Genesis 1 there are various interpretations of this word. In 1:5 there are two interpretations of "day." First, it is contrasted with "night" and then the same word is used to describe a period of time that spans both day and night. Just a few verses later we see a third use of "day". It is the Sabbath day when God rested from all his creating. The Sabbath is called a "yom" as well, even though it is very distinct from all the other days mentioned. Three interpretations of "yom", all in one chapter. That suggests to me that we must not

---

[22] Most scientists date the earth at around 14.5 billion years old.

be too dogmatic about how long we determine these days to be. The Day-Age view provides a good interpretation of "yom".

There is one more interpretation of the creation week we can consider. Scholars have understood the structure of Genesis 1 to be a literary device used to express points of interest in the creation story.[23] The proponents of this, "Framework Theory", will argue that since Genesis is an ancient sacred text and not a scientific textbook, it has a symbolic structure that suggests God designed his creation by creating three expanses and then filling them from first to third. Here is the proposed pattern found in Genesis 1:

- On day one, God created light. On day four he created the *lights* that govern day and night (sun and moon).
- On day two, God created water. On day five he created fish to fill the water.
- On day three, God made dry land. On day six he put animals and humans on the land.
- On the seventh day, God rested. He does this to model how he desires his people to rest one day of the week.

By linking days one and four, two and five, and three and six, the Framework Theory does not want us treating these as literal days but *literary* days. They are poetic. They show God is in control, contrary to other chaotic creation narratives in the ancient world. Lastly, it explains how there could be three days before there was a sun.

Like I said, there are many ways to interpret Genesis 1. We have seen that the text allows for numerous interpretations. Given all the controversy in this area over the years, Christians should be careful how they determine the age of the earth and what we demand of others to believe as well. Augustine would warn us about being too tied to any one view, particularly if it becomes evident that it is contradictory to scientific discovery.

---

[23] D.A. Carson. *The God Who Is There*. (Baker Books, 2010) p14.

WHERE I HAVE LANDED

One of the best books I have read that survey the various interpretations of these highly debated first chapters in Genesis is John Lennox's, *Seven Days That Divide The World*.[24] In an interview about his book, Lennox noted how important it is to understand that Genesis was written in a way that could be understood by all kinds of audiences at all times. He explains:

> If the biblical explanations were at the level, say, of twenty-second century science, it would likely be unintelligible to everyone, including scientists today. This could scarcely have been God's intention. He wished his meaning to be accessible to all.[25]

Chapters 1 and 2 of Genesis do not give us an exhaustive scientific account of how life began. They do, however, give us many clues regarding what God was doing. A creation pattern is evident: God speaks, something happens, God declares it "good", and then time passes before he does it over again.[26] The process repeats itself several times.

The debate becomes merely about timing. How long did it take for God to make everything? My question is: *can anyone be totally sure about that answer?* I can take my guesses based on scientific evidence, but I will certainly not choose to die on any

---

[24] John Lennox. *Seven Days That Divide The World* (Grand Rapids, Mich.: Zondervan, 2010).

[25] Stephanie Samuel. "Can Science, Creationism Coexist? One Christian Author Says 'Yes'" June 19, 2011. Taken from: www.christianpost.com/news/can-science-and-creationism-coexist-one-christian-author-says-yes-51315/. Accessed July 3, 2012.

[26] Lennox notes also that the use of the word "day" is not a specific amount of time but is used flexibly throughout Scripture. I cannot go over all the various arguments or theories here. I can highly recommend Lennox's book as he explores this argument further.

cosmological hill just yet. Furthermore, science does not demand that I do so.

Genesis assures us that the world was not brought forth by random genetic mutation, but by the design and the command of a God who is in full control of the whole process. He is not a "God-of-the-gaps" but a "God-of-the-whole-world." He is the God of what has been discovered and what future scientists will eventually uncover.

I can appreciate a God who begins the creation process and still leaves plenty of room for future scientific discoveries to reveal how that process happened. If nothing else, it keeps unemployment down in the scientific community.

As you may have noticed, I have not landed anywhere in this conversation. For now, I am scientifically agnostic regarding those early days of our existence. What I am confident of is that we have numerous interpretations of Genesis that can accommodate scientific discovery. We are not to become too attached to a reading of Genesis that is tethered to one interpretation of science— that is, unless, as Augustine cautions us, we are prepared to make ourselves look foolish in print.

CONCLUSION

The truth is that science has not disproved the existence of God. Many eminent scientists find that their work and their faith are complementary. Though science cannot give us the meaning of life, morality, love, or any of the other things that mean most to us, we can all learn a great deal about God's world through scientific discovery.

The real tension lies in the way discoveries are reported. How the data are shared reveals something about the presupposition of the one writing the report - whether that person has a particular bias or whether the report is simply a neutral observation of data. Due to differences in worldview, it is understandable that atheistic and theistic scientists will interpret data differently. They will draw from other fields such as psychology, philosophy, or theology. We must all be aware of the biases we bring into all of our work, science included. The church may have a reputation for suppressing scientific discovery but I am confident that this is being corrected today with the high level scholarly work being done by eminent Christians in all fields of science.

Concerning origins, whatever science discovers, we can safely assert that future discoveries will line up with a Creator God. No discovery will ever push him out of the equation. I am convinced that new scientific evidence will reveal to us *how* he made everything. Genesis gives us a great deal of room for interpretation and we readers of the Bible must be humble enough not to be married to an interpretation that is dependent on a dated scientific theory.

The relationship between faith and science is an interesting and complex one and it seems like there are public misunderstandings about how they get along. Once considered, we see that Christians should appreciate and feel free to participate in scientific research. It is my hope that scientists would grow to appreciate the contribution of Christianity in order to develop a well-rounded worldview that explains the world around them, answering life's deepest questions.

THE EVIDENCE FOR GOD - PART ONE:
A FINELY-TUNED UNIVERSE

All nature cries out that there is a Supreme Intelligence.

-Voltaire

For his [God's] invisible attributes, namely, his eternal power and divine nature, have been clearly perceived, ever since the creation of the world, in the things that have been made

-Romans 1:20

Imagine you are flying over the Pacific ocean in one of those little two person planes. The monotony of the endless blue water is all of a sudden broken by what you perceive to be a small, uninhabited island. You take a closer look and notice some letters written in logs on the sand. The four letters are very distinguishable: "H-E-L-P." At this point you have a decision to make. You must decide whether the forces of nature mixed some pieces of driftwood to make the shapes of the letters H, E, L, and

P (in that order) or somebody is in desperate need of rescue and is trying to get your attention. If this word came by random, natural causes, then you need not bother investigating it. If, however, it was the work of someone in trouble, your conscience will obligate you to make sure you help the stranded islander.

There are parallels here to the discovery of letters within human DNA. Within every one of your cells, there a combination of the letters A,C,G and T. These letters form a word out of protein pairs that are responsible for your genetic make up. The different combination of those four letters is called DNA. It is perfectly ordered and responsible for the creation of each and every unique human being on the planet. When we see four letters on a beach, we presume that there is some mind choosing and logically ordering the letters. Knowing there are three and a half billion letters of DNA in a human body, laid out in order, is it such a stretch to apply that same logic as to the stranded islander's message and ask where *it* came from?

The discovery of all the information packed into DNA is one example of how, in recent years, the scientific community has acknowledged the evidence of design on the earth. English physicist Paul Davies wonders if there was some cosmic tinkering going on to allow this.

> There is for me powerful evidence that there is something going on behind it all...it seems as though somebody has fine-tuned nature's numbers to make the Universe...The impression of design is overwhelming.[27]

Was it God who designed everything, or is the appearance of design just a coincidence? In this chapter I will show why I believe God is the best explanation for all the design we observe in the world. I will also show how all alternative naturalistic

---

[27] Paul Davies. *The Cosmic Blueprint*. (New York, Simon And Schuster, 1988) p203.

theories are less compelling than the claim of the Bible that, "In the beginning God created the heavens and the earth" (Gen. 1:1).

GOD IS THE BEST EXPLANATION FOR THE FUNDAMENTAL CONSTANTS

Modern cosmology and physics have revealed several fundamental constants necessary for supporting life. These range from the obvious to the more nuanced and precise. The obvious ones include the distance of the sun from the earth and moon. These necessary distances regulate the Earth's temperature, tides, seasons, gravity, etc. For instance, the sun is 93 million miles from the earth. If it were any closer to the earth, our planet would be too hot to support any kind of life on it. If the earth were any further from the sun, as well as the moon, we would all freeze to death. Secondly, because of Earth's precise positioning from the sun, the gravitational pull from the sun and our moon controls the ocean's tides and currents. The size and distance of sun, moon and earth along with the force of gravity keep the earth on a 23.5 degree axis. Without this we would lose our seasons and be devastated by regular tsunamis.

Furthermore, the expansion level of the universe balances perfectly with the force of gravity. Francis Collins has noted the importance of a fine-tuned gravitational force. He writes:

> It turns out that if we change gravity by even a tiny fraction of a percent—enough so that you would be, say, one billionth of a gram heavier or lighter—the universe becomes so different that there are no stars, galaxies, or planets.[28]

Such precise laws of gravity are necessary in order to prevent the universe from collapsing on itself. This was of particular importance in the early days of our universe.

---

[28] Francis Collins. "What Is Fine-Tuning?" www.biologos.org/questions/fine-tuning. Accessed May 2, 2012.

John Jefferson Davis has looked at the precise, necessary fundamentals just to accommodate these initial moments. He concluded that an accuracy of one part in 10^{60} was needed to keep the universe intact during those initial moments of the universe's existence. He compares this to firing a bullet at a one-inch target on the other side of the observable universe, twenty billion light years away, and hitting it right in the middle.[29] Perhaps a shot like that could happen, but would anybody bid on it? Nevertheless, many skeptics are basing their souls on such chance.

With more time, we would consider other constants that had to be present simultaneously for our cosmos to even take its "first steps" forward. I am talking about the laws of entropy, the balanced ratio of the nuclear strong-force to electromagnetic force, and others. All of these constants, which appear to be fine-tuned and hang on the razor's edge of precision,[30] provide an inductive platform on which to build the second piece of evidence in support of God's existence—the presence of observable information.

GOD IS THE BEST EXPLANATION FOR
THE PRESENCE OF OBSERVABLE INFORMATION

Could a thousand monkeys writing on a thousand typewriters produce the works of Shakespeare? This classic question called the *Infinite Monkey Theorem,* was put to the test in 2003 when a group of English research students from Plymouth University put six Sulawesi crested macaques (a.k.a. "monkeys") in a

[29] John Jefferson Davis. "The Design Argument, Cosmic Fine-Tuning, and the Anthropic Principle." *The International Journal of Philosophy and Religion* 22 (1987) p. 140

[30] Physicist Paul Davies points out that if the nuclear strong force had been different by one part in 10^{16}, no stars could have formed and no life would be possible. See Davies, Paul. *God and the New Physics* (London, JM Dent and Sons, 1983).

monitored room with a computer.[31] The goal was simple: observe what kind of literature these monkeys could generate.

What were the results? "They pressed a lot of 'S,'" remarked researcher Mike Phillips. Phillips also noted the monkey's preference of the A, J, L and M keys as well. This was not the kind of literature for which the research students were hoping. Even more disappointing, the literary experiment degenerated quickly as the leader monkeys began smashing the computer with nearby inanimate objects. If that weren't enough, the researchers also documented the strange habit the monkeys developed of urinating and defecating on the keyboard.

If the six monkeys couldn't arrange five letters on a keyboard, how could random genetic mutation create not only the four letters we find in DNA but also arrange them in such a way as to organize all living things? According to DNA researchers like Stephen Meyer and Francis Collins, coincidence cannot explain all the information found in DNA. To these scientists at the very top of their fields, the existence of God is the best explanation for the information found in DNA.

In 2009, Stephen C. Meyer wrote a book called *Signature In The Cell*[32] with the sole purpose of explaining the link between the existence of God and his findings as a top level biologist. If there is information in DNA necessary for creating and sustaining life, Meyer argues, then someone must have put it there.

Elsewhere Meyer writes, "living systems display tell-tale signs of actual or 'intelligent' design such as the presence of complex circuits, miniature motors and digital information in living cells." In the same article, he adds:

---

[31] Jill Lawless. "Typing Monkeys Just Make Mess." Vancouver Sun. Associated Press. May 10, 2003.

[32] Stephen C. Meyer. *Signature In The Cell*. (Harper Collins, 2009).

DNA functions like a software program. We know that software comes from programmers. Information — whether inscribed in hieroglyphics, written in a book, or encoded in a radio signal — always arises from a designing intelligence. So the discovery of digital code in DNA provides a strong scientific reason for concluding that the information in DNA also had an intelligent source.[33]

Francis Collins was once an atheist, but his scientific research led him to abandon his atheist beliefs. After winning the Nobel Prize for *The Human Genome Project*, the project where his team mapped out human DNA, Collins said in a statement, "It is humbling for me and awe-inspiring to realize that we have caught the first glimpse of our own instruction book, previously known only to God."[34]

To date, evolutionists have not been able to come up with any sort of biologically reasonable or workable explanation as to how the first cell evolved. Michael Behe's lifework has been to show that such cells loaded with information are "irreducibly complex" and that it is impossible for DNA to have evolved in sequence.[35] Critics of Behe offer *alternative explanations* as to how such complexity could have evolved but are unable to actually recreate such an occurrence themselves. Some suggest that since science will eventually show how natural selection made it happen, explanations do not have to be given today. This "Darwin-of-the-Gaps" approach is acceptable as an alternative explanation to how God may have accomplished it, but it still requires a large faith statement to say that it all happened by an unguided, chance process.

---

[33] Stephen Meyer. "Pro-Darwin Consensus Doesn't Rule Out Intelligent Design." http://www.discovery.org/a/13391. Accessed May 2012.

[34] Francis Collins. Said in a public statement in June, 2000. www.news.bbc.co.uk. Accessed March 2010.

[35] Check out *Darwin's Black Box* and *Edge Of Evolution*.

The fact that there is ordered, intelligent, and systematic information in DNA gives us strong evidence that there was first an intelligent designer who put it there. The alternative is too much of a leap in the dark for me and scientists like Meyer and Collins.

GOD IS THE BEST EXPLANATION FOR
THE ORDER OF MATHEMATICS

Nobel Laureate mathematician, Eugene Wigner, was surprised to find so many dependable constants in mathematics. He described this as, "the unreasonable effectiveness of mathematics."[36] Wigner acknowledged the "mysterious" connection that mathematics has with the natural sciences adding that "there is no rational explanation for it."[37] Adding to Wigner's inability to explain the orderliness of mathematics, atheist philosopher, Bertrand Russell, saw beauty in it. He wrote in his essay, *A Study of Mathematics*:

> Mathematics, rightly viewed, possesses not only truth, but supreme beauty; beauty cold and austere, like that of sculpture, without appeal to any part of our weaker nature, without the gorgeous trappings of painting or music...The true spirit of delight, the exaltation, the sense of being more than man, which is the touchstone of the highest excellence, is to be found in mathematics as surely as in poetry.[38]

---

[36] Eugene Wigner. "The Unreasonable Effectiveness of Mathematics in the Natural Sciences,". Taken from *Communications in Pure and Applied Mathematics*, (Vol. 13, No. I, New York, February,1960).

[37] Eugene Wigner. "The Unreasonable Effectiveness of Mathematics", Communications in Pure and Applied Mathematics, 13 (1960).

[38] Bertrand Russell. "*A Study Of Mathematics*." Printed in *Philosophical Essays*, (London, England, 1967).

Russell saw beauty in the laws of math and likened them to the beauty he saw in other forms of art such as sculpture, painting, music, and poetry. Though these comparisons all demand an artist, it is curious to note that Russell concluded that there was still no Designer behind Earth's natural art!

Western science was founded on the idea that mathematics is not some collection of chaotic forces but rather that God had made an orderly universe that could be studied by human beings. Because God was the creator and sustainer of the world, scientists can trust that the world they study today will still be the world we can know tomorrow.

In 1964, Peter Higgs, using mathematics, theorized that within every cell, an undiscovered particle existed. After more than forty years, countless man hours, and millions of dollars expended, evidence of the Higgs-Boson particle (or more sensationally known as the, "God-particle") was discovered by scientists in 2012. It is amazing to think that a theoretical mathematical equation in the 1960s could lead to the discovery of a boson particle otherwise unseen or unknown but for the clues found in mathematics. I believe the best explanation for the presence and efficacy of mathematics is God.

ALTERNATIVE EXPLANATIONS THAT JUST DON'T EXPLAIN ENOUGH

Richard Dawkins states that, "Biology is the study of complicated things that give the appearance of having been designed for a purpose."[39] Though the appearance of design is evident, that does not persuade everyone to concede of a Designer. Natural selection, skeptics will argue, is a process that

---

[39] Richard Dawkins. *The Blind Watchmaker* (New York: W. W. Norton & Company, 1996) p.1

will find a way to ensure life happens.[40] They say this in order to be consistent with their commitment to the naturalistic worldview.

To avoid admitting a Designer is involved, skeptics theorize that there exist *multiple* universes of which our universe is the lucky one.[41] This is known as the "multiverse theory."

A Finely-Tuned Multiverse Generator

The multiverse theory supposes that, given an infinite number of potential parallel universes, one is sure to generate a life-sustaining universe such as ours.

Some philosophers argue that we should not be surprised that we can make observations about our universe's finely-tuned ability to support life. After all, we are living here. "Of course our universe can support life! We are alive to talk about it," they will say. To them, there is no need to talk of design or of God. Our universe is simply a result of the law of averages working out in our favour. In every lottery, they will argue, regardless of how improbable the odds of winning are, *somebody* is going to win the draw. We, in our universe, just happened to win our lottery. Given enough universes generated, and with enough time, one like ours is bound to be actualized. That, to skeptics, will be enough speculation to keep them satisfied in order to avoid acknowledging a fine-tuner, namely, God.

Regardless of whether research goes on to either confirm or deny the existence of multiverses, the results will still be insufficient as an argument against God's existence. An unprecedented event such as a multiverse discovery will simply move the skeptic's problem back one step: *Who makes the multiverses?* If a multiverse

---

[40] Richard Dawkins. *The God Delusion* (Bantam Press, London, 2006). See also Dawkins', *The Selfish Gene* and *The Blind Watchmaker*.

[41] David Deutsch. *The Fabric Of Reality* (London, Penguin Books, 1997).

generator is responsible for the existence of multiple universes, who or what is responsible for the existence of the multiverse generator? Even a multiverse generating machine would need to be finely tuned to pump out new universes. If the multiverse theory is ever conceded, the theist can rest on the fact that it is God who fine-tuned the multiverse generator.

Quantum theorist, John Polkinghorne provides a sober perspective about multiverses in his book, *One World*:

> Let us recognize these speculations for what they are. They are not physics, but in the strictest sense, metaphysics. There is no purely scientific reason to believe in an ensemble of universes. By construction these other worlds are unknowable by us. A possible explanation of equal intellectual respectability – and to my mind greater economy and elegance – would be that this one world is the way it is, because it is the creation of the will of a Creator who purposes that it should be so.[42]

Polkinghorne rejects the multiverse interpretation of his contemporaries. To him, it is too speculative and even outside of the realm of physics to accept as scientifically responsible. Oxford philosopher Richard Swinburne takes it further. "To postulate a trillion-trillion other universes, rather than one God, in order to explain the orderliness of our universe, seems the height of irrationality."[43]

The Chances of a Universe Happening by Chance

Scientist, Dr. Freeman Dyson admits, "There are many...lucky accidents in physics." The question can be asked, "Just how *lucky* does the universe have to be in order to exist as it does?" If it

---

[42] John Polkinghorne. *One World*, (London, Eng. : SPCK, 1986) p. 80

[43] Richard Swinburne. *Is There a God?* (Oxford, Eng.: Oxford University Press, 1995), p. 68

could be shown that it was chance that caused the fine-tuning of the universe, this argument would fail. What kind of chance are we talking about?[44]

In 1989, Oxford mathematician, Roger Penrose calculated the precision necessary to create a universe with the various constants which would be suitable for life. [45] He claimed that the probability of a universe coming into existence by chance is one part in $10^{(10 \text{ to the power of } 123)}$.[46]

Since these numbers are so incomprehensibly small, many analogies have been offered to show the improbability that the universe we observe came about by such "luck."

The most helpful analogy I have heard came when I had the opportunity to interview Dr. William Lane Craig. Dr. Craig envisioned a situation in which you are captured by some kidnappers who have every intent to kill you. Before you are executed, the captors insist on playing a little game with your life. The kidnappers take you into a huge warehouse full of *billions and billions and billions* of black ping pong balls. They pull one white ping pong ball out of their pocket and throw it into the pile of black ones. Mixed well into the billions, your captors tell you that if their random-ball-selecting machine chooses the white ball, you will live. Your heart sinks. You know your chances of getting that ball among the countless black balls is less than minuscule. You say your final prayers in preparation

---

[44] See the full argument in Freeman Dyson's book *Disturbing The Universe* (New York, NY: Harper & Row, 1979) p. 251.

[45] Roger Penrose. *The Emperor's New Mind.* (Oxford, Eng.:Oxford University Press, 1989).

[46] This is 10 followed by 10^{123} zeros. If we were to actually try and write this number out, there would not be enough particles in the entire known universe to accomplish the task. The paper costs would be literally out of this world.

for the worst. The machine starts up. It hovers around the warehouse, and to your surprise, comes out with the white ball!

Phew...Your life has been spared, and the game is over. You start to walk proudly out of the warehouse.

"Not so fast," grin the kidnappers as they pull you back. "It has to choose the white ball four more times."

Feeling betrayed, you are forced to watch as the white ball goes back in among the billions and is mixed around again. If a black ball is chosen, your life is over. But wait - the white ball is picked again...and again...and again...and yet again. In complete disbelief at what has just happened, your captors throw up their hands, forced now to release you. "What a stupid idea that was!" said one of them hitting his friend up-side the head.

Yes, the possibility is there, but does anyone actually believe that kind of improbability is possible? Notre Dame philosopher, Dr. Alvin Plantinga, uses the illustration of an anomalous poker game where the dealer deals himself four aces for twenty straight hands in a row. When questioned, the dealer *could* logically argue that given an infinite number of possible universes, it is *possible* that there is a universe in which four aces could be dealt twenty straight times. And, he could argue, in such a universe, there is no need to suspect anyone of cheating. Unconvinced, the rest of the card players reach for their six shooters. It is obvious that though the dealer's argument is possible, such an argument will not be accepted in *their* universe.[47]

You have to place yourself somewhere in Plantinga's story. Are you the dealer pleading for the once-in-a-million lifetimes chance, or are you the guys chasing him out of town knowing that it never really happens? There is one other point made by

---

[47] Alvin Plantinga. "Dennett's Dangerous Idea" in *Books And Culture* (May 1996). p35.

one famous skeptic that should be addressed before I conclude this chapter.

DID ANYONE DESIGN THE DESIGNER?

Richard Dawkins points out that the theist's fine-tuning argument is not without its own shortcomings. In the most forceful, self-admitted God-defeating chapter of his best selling book, *The God Delusion*, Dawkins asks, "If theists want to say there is a cosmic designer, who designed the designer?" He continues, "the theist's answer is unsatisfying because it leaves the existence of God unexplained..."

Reading this, I am puzzled that such a smart man can make so much money with such a bad argument. Dawkins' demand here is unreasonable. One needs to ask the question of "who made God" only if one believes God can be made. The idea of a God who must be created is indeed a delusion. The book of Isaiah is comically critical of anyone who creates a god for himself (see Isaiah 44:9-17). If Dawkins titled his book, *The Created God Delusion*, he could have used far fewer words and had the full agreement of Christians on his side![48]

The theist needs to give no explanation for the origin of God to conclude that God is the best explanation for the finely-tuned universe we observe. Not all statements demand explanations in order for them to be held as valid. If this were the case, to demand such would be to demand infinite layers of explanations upon explanations.

In my opening example about the stranded islander, I do not have to know all about the person who put the sticks in place in order to conclude that it was a real person who did it. I do not need to know his name, hometown, parents or anything other than the fact that those sticks look like a word too complex to be

---

[48] Thanks to John Lennox for help on this cheeky little point.

created by a chance positioning of driftwood by the wind and waves.

It follows that the theist does not need to answer the "Who designed God?" question in order to observe fine-tuning in the universe and conclude that God fine-tuned it. Dawkins' main point in *The God Delusion* turns out to be no point at all. The theist believes that God is eternal. He is outside of our ticking *chronos* time and completely separate from the world he made. The theist looks at fundamental constants that support human life and concludes that they are far too precise to come about by random chance.

CONCLUSION

Continuing on with the illustration about flying your plane over a seemingly uninhabited island, imagine this situation: the debris you saw doesn't say "HELP" but rather "This message came about by chance." That would be helpful, wouldn't it? It made your decision easy. You do not have to stop your flight and save anyone. After all, the message clearly came from nothing. Then again, is that really even possible? Regardless of what the message said, we would be foolish to think that such a well-structured sentence came from random wind and tidal forces colliding with rocks and wood.

The impression of a world with design is noticeable by theists and atheists alike. I have argued that the finely-tuned constants necessary for the existence of our universe, our earth and human life are extremely compelling evidence for God's existence. I have also explained how the appearance of information in DNA, order in mathematics plus our ability to understand math is further evidence that God is the best explanation. In this chapter, I have also shown how a skeptic's alternative explanations such as an appeal to chance, or hypothetical multiverses are all insufficient counter-arguments against God's existence.

In the end, Edward Harrison says the final choice is all of ours to make.

> Take your choice: blind chance that requires multitudes of universes, or design that requires only one... Many scientists, when they admit their views, incline towards the design argument.[49]

These scientists Harrison mentions *should* incline towards design. Things that have the strong appearance of design usually are designed by someone. As we can recognize human design in art, music, and architecture, so too can we recognize the work of a master with math, physics, sunsets and everything else that makes the anomaly of the very Earth we live on so beautiful. This, to me, is some of the most compelling evidence for the existence of God.

Thankfully, it is not the only piece of compelling evidence we have. There is much more yet to consider.

---

[49] Edward Harrison. *Masks Of The Universe* (New York, NY.: Macmillan, 1985). p252.

THE EVIDENCE FOR GOD - PART TWO:
THE BIG BANGER

"No philosophical theory which I have yet come across is a radical improvement on the words of Genesis, that 'In the beginning God made Heaven and Earth.'"

-C.S. Lewis

"What if God doesn't actually exist?"

I do not even remember when this kind of questioning started going through my head. It was sometime during puberty. That is the span of my life when most of my troubles started happening. At this point the words, "just believe" no longer seemed like a good enough reason to accept the idea of God's existence. I wanted to know that there were good reasons to believe that the God everyone at church was always talking about was actually real.

In Grade 12 I took a public speaking class. For two weeks we learned about debating. The final project assigned to us was to debate another student on any topic of our choosing. A friend and I decided to debate the existence of God. I figured that if I could learn enough to publicly debate someone about God's existence, I could probably figure out if I really believed it or not. If at the end I had no reasons to believe in God, my friend would win the debate, and my questions about God would be answered. During my preparation time, I found the cosmological argument the most compelling evidence for the existence of God. Many years later, this is still the one I go to when I am struggling with doubt. Let me explain why I found it so helpful as a Grade 12 student and still today as one devoted to helping people see the evidence for believing in God.

THE ONLY THREE OPTIONS

The beauty of the cosmological argument for the existence of God is that it is incredibly simple. It seeks to answer the question that has swirled in the minds of philosophers for many centuries. The eighteenth century philosopher, Gottfried Leibniz is credited with asking the question "Why is there something rather than nothing?"

When it comes to the question of the origins of our universe, there are really only three options for Leibniz concerning what happened back then:

1. The universe popped into existence.
2. The universe has always existed.
3. God created the universe.

Here I want to show why I think it is most reasonable to believe it was the third option - God created the universe. We will start by process of elimination on the first two possibilities.

1. Can a Universe Appear out of Nothing, from Nothing?

If the universe just popped into existence, it would violate all the laws of physics. The Law of Cause and Effect states that every effect must first have a direct cause. We know this to be true because in our everyday world, things do not ever "just happen." If you start with nothing, you get nothing. If you put no money into a bank account, you will have no money at the end of the month. You will generate no interest— neither from girls nor from your bank.

Not everyone sees it this way. University of Cambridge Professor, Dr. Stephen Hawking, has suggested that gravity is the best explanation for the creation of the universe. It sounds smart coming from an academic like Hawking, but could it work practically? What is gravity? Gravity is a law that explains how physical matter behaves. What can a law create? As my scrappy Irish professor, Dr. John Lennox, liked to say, "Two and two may equal four but two plus two has never put four dollars in my pocket." Logic tells us that X can create Y, but X cannot create X. Logic tells us that the universe cannot create itself. Again I have heard Dr. Lennox add here, "Nonsense remains nonsense even when it is said by smart people."

We well know that out of nothing, nothing comes. It we started with nothing, we would have nothing to show for it. That's what nothing does— *nothing*. Since the universe could not have appeared from nothing, that leaves us with two more options: either the universe has always existed or God made it.

2. Has the Universe Always Existed?

It is a fascinating story how the scientific community came to accept the current theories regarding the age of the universe. Since Aristotle, it has been widely believed that our known universe has always existed. Enlightenment skeptics laughed at those who insisted the Bible's claim that "In the beginning God made the heavens and the earth" was an intellectually credible statement. Today, however, it is widely accepted that our universe indeed had a beginning. Dr. Stephen Hawking, an expert in cosmology states:

> All the evidence seems to indicate that the universe has not existed forever, but that it had a beginning, about fifteen billion years ago. This is probably the most remarkable discovery of modern cosmology.[50]

Let me explain this remarkable discovery that Hawking referenced.

The idea that the universe had a beginning was a twentieth century scientific discovery. It emerged as a result of observations in the structure of the universe and theoretical physics. Building on the work of Albert Einstein, Alexander Friedmann and Edwin Hubble (after whom we have named the famous telescope), it was the work of a Roman Catholic priest who made the discovery that Stephen Hawking found so remarkable.

Georges Lemaître was a devout Catholic priest. However, he had many other credentials. This priest was also a world class physicist trained at Cambridge, Harvard and MIT. He took his scientific work as seriously as he conducted his clerical duties. I included his role as a priest just in case you had forgotten that those who did church work could still participate in scientific discussions. In the 1920s and 30s, Dr. Lemaître's research was going against the prevailing eternal universe model of Aristotle. Lemaître observed that the reason for an ever expanding

---

[50] Stephen Hawking. "The Beginning Of Time". www.hawking.org.uk/the-beginning-of-time.html. Accessed May 19, 2012.

universe was best explained by tracing everything back to a single reference point.[51]

According to his calculations, the universe began with a quantum explosion approximately fourteen billion years ago.[52] After the early expansion of hot, dense matter, everything cooled in order to allow energy to be converted to subatomic particles like protons, neutrons and electrons.

As a physicist, Georges Lemaître had many critics. They criticized his science, suspecting a religious motivation behind his research. If his "hypothesis of the primeval atom"[53] (as he called it) was accepted, this would be an enormous gain to the claims of Genesis 1 in the Bible. It was these very claims that many scientists in those days were trying to avoid.

Lemaître's theory was adamantly opposed by atheist and critic of the church, Professor Fred Hoyle. Hoyle coined the term "That Big Bang" in the media in an effort to ridicule Lemaître and others who were being won over to the idea that the universe had a beginning. To Hoyle, this theory smelled

---

[51] Georges Lemaître. "A Homogeneous Universe of Constant Mass and Growing Radius Accounting for the Radial Velocity of Extragalactic Nebulae". *Monthly Notices of the Royal Astronomical Society*, 1931. p483–490.

[52] Of course, this figure is debatable. I'm using NASA's estimates based on scientific research. See article "What Is The Age Of The Universe" (*Age of the Universe*. The National Aeronautics and Space Administration (NASA). Accessed December 12, 2012). Elsewhere in this book I have argued that Genesis 1 allows us to simply follow the science wherever it leads us regarding the age of the earth.

[53] Georges Lemaître. "The Beginning of the World from the Point of View of Quantum Theory", *Nature* (Volume 127, 1931), p. 706.

suspiciously like a distinctly Christian idea that had religious implications.[54]

Albert Einstein was at first critical of Lemaître's work. After several years of dialoguing with Lemaître, Einstein eventually came to accept the priest's cosmological theory. Following one of Lemaître's lectures, Einstein is said to have stood up, applauded loudly and exclaimed, "This is the most beautiful and satisfactory explanation of creation to which I have ever listened."[55] Lemaître was excelling through the peer review process, with Einstein jumping on his proverbial cosmological bandwagon.

Several decades after he first proposed the theory, and by the time the Second World War was over, the *Big Bang Theory*, as it came to be known, was widely accepted in scientific fields. Today it is the working theory upon which all other cosmological understanding is built.

Such monumental discoveries like that of Georges Lemaître were worthy of a Nobel Prize. In honour of his achievement, I drew the following cartoon.

---

[54] See article, "Big Bang Astronomer Dies." BBC News. August 22, 2001. www.news.bbc.co.uk/2/hi/uk_news/1503721.stm Accessed March 12, 2013.

[55] Charles Van Doren. *A History Of Knowledge* (USA, Random House Publishing, 1991). p334

A JOURNEY TO THE TOP

One morning, three scientists broke out of their lab and planned a hike. It was a hike that no human had ever made before - they would be the first to climb to the top of Mount Reasonable.

Not many dared to venture where these scientists were going.

Not knowing if they would ever be back, they began their long and dangerous trek.

They approached a yellow wood and came to a split in the path. Thankfully, they had a map with them. It instructed them to turn left on a road less travelled.

They took that road...and it made all the difference.

As the road turned into steep cliffs. It became apparent why so few ever ventured this way.

With the sun about to set, the scientists knew they would have to find a spot to sleep.

The scientists found a flat place to rest, cook some dinner, and sleep for the night.

In the morning they would make the last push to the top of Mount Reasonable.

The next morning, conditions worsened as they got closer to the top.

The scientists slipped only a few times but got back up right away and kept climbing. Each kept himself motivated with thoughts of being the first people to ever reach the top.

Breaking over the last cliff, the scientists reached the pinnacle.

They had actually accomplished what everyone else thought impossible.

Then came the biggest surprise of the whole journey.

At the top of Mount Reasonable stood Moses and a bunch of Hebrews.

The Hebrews welcomed the scientists with open arms, and a hand up. It wasn't such a new discovery after all.

THE END

The beginning of our universe is an important discovery for what is called the "Kalam Cosmological Argument" for the existence of God, promoted by philosopher and theologian, Dr. William Lane Craig. It is helpful to understand and easy to remember. It goes like this:

1. Whatever begins to exist has a cause.
2. The universe began to exist.
3. Therefore, the universe has a cause.

Note that, "Everything that begins to exist" excludes God. In the last chapter, we learned that since God is eternal, he has no beginning. Since God is a being that exists outside of time, he is the one who could create time. This is a reasonable claim to make. What is unreasonable is to think that time can create itself. G.K. Chesterton once wrote, "It is absurd for the skeptic to complain that it is unthinkable for God to make everything out of nothing, and then pretend that it is more thinkable that nothing should turn itself into anything."[56]

The Possibility of Multiple Universes as an Explanation

Skeptics, unwilling to concede to the idea of God, the uncaused Causer, have put forward various alternative string, quantum, multiverse and oscillating universe theories. These were investigated more in depth in the last chapter and are, we must remember, simply alternative explanations. The existence of multiple universes parallel to ours is merely a metaphysical *possibility*. That is, these lie outside of the testable realm of physics and are far from being proven.

Those who insist that God has no part in the origin of the universe are backed into the multiverse corner with nowhere else to go. Rather than concede that God is the best explanation for our beginnings, they must come up with metaphysical ideas that cannot be proven by science. It is curious that this is often the kind of blind faith of which theists are always being accused.

Furthermore (and I am cautious to concede such a hypothetical point), should a hypothesis such as the existence of multiverses ever become evident, this only pushes the cause-effect question back one step. We will then again have to ask, "Where did the multiverses get their start?" Every thing that begins to exist must have a cause. What caused the existence of multiverses?

---

[56] G.K. Chesterton. *St. Thomas Aquinas: "The Dumb Ox"*. First published, 1933.

We are back to Leibniz's earlier question: "Why is there something rather than nothing?" The evidence shows that "In the beginning God" is still the best answer.

WHAT KIND OF CREATOR IS THIS?

Whatever begins to exist must have a cause. Our universe, it has been shown, began to exist. Therefore, the universe has a cause. The Causer of this cause must have certain characteristics we can now determine. This Causer had to be:

- *Eternal.* It had to be outside of time since it is responsible for creating time. Logically, you cannot make time if you are restricted within time.
- *Spiritual.* It must be made of a substance that is outside of physical space since it made everything that exists within our understanding of space.
- *Uncaused.* Whatever begins to exist has a cause. Whatever is eternal must begin all causes. It is similar to someone or something that must be outside of the standing dominoes in order to knock the first one over.
- *Immaterial.* It had to create material in the first place.
- *Personal.* A choice had to be made when to begin everything. An impersonal force like the wind or gravity cannot make decisions like this. At a moment of its own choosing, a personal being must make the decision when to create everything.[57]

I believe God is the best explanation for the eternal, spiritual, uncaused, immaterial, and personal being that gave us our universe.

CONCLUSION

---

[57] Craig, William Lane. Reasonable Faith. (Wheaton, ILL Crossway Books, 2008). p93-157.

Concerning origins, we have seen that there were only three options regarding why there is something rather than nothing. Either the universe popped into existence, the universe has always existed, or God created the universe.

I have shown that the universe could not have just "popped" into existence since this would be a violation of the laws of physics. We know that out of nothing, nothing comes. It is like this every time.

Secondly, scientific evidence suggests that the universe has not always existed, but as the Bible has been saying for centuries and science has revealed for decades, our universe had a beginning.

This leaves us with only one option left: God is the eternal, spiritual, uncaused, immaterial, and personal, Banger of the Big Bang. This is, I believe, the most rational explanation for why there is something rather than nothing.

Coupled with the design argument of the previous chapter, we now have two solid pieces of evidence why believing in a Creator God is the best explanation for the world in which we live.

We still haven't looked at the one argument that was enough to turn my hero, C.S. Lewis, from an atheist to a man who believed wholeheartedly in the existence of God. We will cover that one next.

THE EVIDENCE FOR GOD - PART THREE:
OBJECTIVE MORALITY

"The most valued attributes of mankind do not come naturally to the human animal; character borrows from the divine."

-A.S.A. Jones

The ages of eighteen to thirty are filled with many choices. During this time we decide which career path to walk, which university to attend, where we will live, and who/if we will marry. We will make choices that involve our finances, our clothes, our friends, our sexuality and many more. Some will be good choices, and others we will wish we could try again. It will not be hard to gain a consensus of people who agree with the premise that some choices we make are right, and some are wrong. We just have to look at a bad elementary school hair cut for confirmation of this. Some choices are far more disastrous than just a bad bowl cut. For instance, is it ever right for a gunman to choose to enter an elementary school and shoot little boys and girls? Of course not. What I want to ask in this chapter is: Why do you think that it is wrong to do that? Where do you get that sense of morality?

The idea that it is always wrong to murder innocent boys and girls is what we call an "objective moral value." The belief that it is always right to be brave, to tell the truth and to stand up against bullies is what is called an "objective moral duty." My assumption is that most sane people live like these values and duties are true but struggle to understand where morality comes from when they are asked. The fact that these objective moral values and duties exist is further evidence for the existence of God.

Leaning on the work of Dr. William Lane Craig, my argument will look like this:

> 1. If God does not exist, objective moral values and duties do not exist.
> 2. Objective moral values and duties do exist.
> 3. Therefore, God exists.[58]

Let's look at each premise individually.

NO GOD, NO MORALITY?

The first premise of this argument can be summarized, "If God does not exist, neither does objective morality." If God does not exist, where do we get the sense of any foundation for right and wrong? There are a few theories out there.

Some people think that we should base our behaviour upon the habits of our predecessors in the animal kingdom. I have heard a university student make a case for accepting adultery based on the mating habits of hyenas and primates. I hope that student

---

[58]Here I lean heavily on the work of Dr. William Lane Craig for this argument. See *On Guard* (Grand Rapids, Mich.: Zondervan, 2010). p. 129-131.

either smartens up or never gets married. His family would be destroyed with that kind of thinking.

A common explanation for morality is that human beings can craft a moral framework for our behaviour based on Darwinian natural selection. Natural selection reasons like this, "If this is how the animals behave(d), this explains why we can/do behave as well."

Even Darwin was confused about the foundation of human morality. He wrote in *The Descent of Man*:

> If...men were reared under precisely the same conditions as hive-bees, there can hardly be a doubt that our unmarried females would, like the worker-bees, think it a sacred duty to kill their brothers, and mothers would strive to kill their fertile daughters, and no one would think of interfering.[59]

A university student once told me that homo sapiens have adapted the morality of being civil with each other in order to propagate the human species. They enter into a social contract where people look out for each other's good in order to survive. This reasoning is not only contrary to Darwinian "survival of the fittest" (think what Darwin said about the ethics of bees), but it also suggests that all acts of love are done "purely" out of self interest. Darwin knew that natural selection had limits in its ability to explain human behaviour. For instance, "survival of the fittest" cannot explain why a person does good deeds with no advantage to himself or herself.[60] When people give to the *Red Cross* to help tsunami victims on the other side of the world, when someone selflessly volunteers their time and talents working with the poor, or when an upper-middle class family

---

[59] Charles Darwin. *The Descent Of Man and Selection in Relation To Sex*, 2nd Edition. (New York , NY. : D. Appleton and Company, 1909), p100.

[60] Francis Collins. *The Language Of God* (New York, NY: Simon and Schuster, 2006). p27.

adopts an African child, the Darwinian is left scratching his or her head.

These examples and other common sacrificial acts of service that we hear about every day often have no biological advantage to the DNA of the one making the sacrifice. To assume that their motive was to propagate their DNA would be insulting and demeaning to the heroism of their sacrifice.

How Honest Atheists Feel About Morality

I give credit to Richard Dawkins' integrity for putting in print the moral conclusions of his atheistic worldview. I say this because most atheists I speak with are not willing to go that far. In *River Out Of Eden,* Dawkins willingly admits,

> In a universe of blind physical forces and genetic replication, some people are going to get hurt, other people are going to get lucky, and you won't find any rhyme or reason in it, nor any justice. The universe we observe has precisely the properties we should expect if there is, at bottom, no design, no purpose, no evil and no good, nothing but blind pitiless indifference.[61]

Professor Dawkins gets this from reflecting on the random chances he perceives in the movement of electrons. This is merely evidence of his scientific reductionism based on a worldview that does not include God. Dawkins looks at a cell and finds no instruction manual or game plan for how things should go. Consider what Dawkins' colleague, Dr. Stephen Jay Gould, has said about the process by which atheists draw such conclusions:

> We are here because one odd group of fishes had a peculiar fin anatomy that could transform into legs for terrestrial

---

[61] Richard Dawkins. *River Out Of Eden* (Oxford, Eng.: Bantam Press, 1995). p133.

creatures; because the earth never froze entirely during an ice age; because a small and tenuous species, arising in Africa a quarter of a million years ago, has managed, so far, to survive by hook and by crook. We may yearn for a "higher" answer but none exists.[62]

Given atheism, it is tough to find any deeper meaning than the story that Gould is telling here: "Don't waste your time looking for any higher answers or deeper meaning. You will not find any."

Can We Be Good Without God?

Twelve times out of ten when sharing this I will hear the rebuttal, "I'm an atheist. Are you saying that I'm not a good person?" It is always the nicest people who ask this. That is, they are nice people who have misunderstood my argument. I never question an atheist's ability to do good things, nor their ability to recognize goodness when they see it in others. I am only asking about the foundation where their idea of goodness comes from.

Think about goodness like you think about gravity. Whether or not you believe in gravity, it is still there. Every day you are affected by gravity regardless of how well you understand the physics of it. In this chapter I am asking whether objective morality is something like gravity operating in accordance with the laws of the universe. Are there some things that are always right and some things that are always wrong? Put another way, has there ever been a time in history where it would have been acceptable for Hitler to kill over five million Jews? Or is mass murder *always* wrong no matter when or where you are? If mass murder is always wrong, then it turns out that objective moral values and duties do exist.

---

[62] James Haught. *2000 Years of Disbelief, Famous People with the Courage to Doubt* (Amherst, NY.: Prometheus Books, 1996).

Philosopher Richard Taylor exposes the common mistake atheists make as they assume a *foundation* of morality that exists apart from God. He explains,

> The modern age, more or less repudiating the idea of a divine lawgiver, has nevertheless tried to retain the ideas of moral right and wrong, not noticing that, in casting God aside, they have also abolished the conditions of meaningfulness for moral right and wrong as well. Thus, even educated persons sometimes declare things as war, or abortion, or the violation of certain human rights, are "morally wrong," and they imagine that they have said something true and significant. *Educated people do not need to be told, however, that questions such as these have never been answered outside of religion*...Contemporary writers in ethics, who blithely discourse upon moral right and wrong and moral obligation without any reference to religion, are really just weaving intellectual webs from thin air; which amounts to saying that they discourse without meaning.[63]

To summarize Taylor's view, atheists who argue that there could exist an objective morality without God are like vegans who still want their burgers to taste like meat. These are people who have made their choice but are having a hard time accepting the consequences.

I have shown that if backed up only by the process of evolution or the worldview of atheism, premise one of the moral argument still stands: *If God does not exist, objective moral values and duties do not exist.*

OBJECTIVE MORAL VALUES AND DUTIES *DO* EXIST

---

[63] Richard Taylor. *Ethics, Faith And Reason* (Englewood Cliffs, CA : Prentice-Hall, 1985).

Premise two of the moral argument for the existence of God depends on showing that objective, moral values and duties that we all know and try to live by do exist.

Demonstrating that objective morality exists is relatively easy, but proving it can be quite difficult. We all believe that human beings should not be able to do whatever they want, to whomever they want, whenever they want. Perception tells us of a law of "rights" and "wrongs" and "shoulds" that apply to everyone no matter where they are in the world, who their government is, or what religion they follow. We know Hitler was wrong, that it is always wrong to torture children, or to rape a person, or sleep with another man's wife. That is why we have laws and a justice system that punishes people for breaking these laws. These are the wrongs that know no international or historic borders.

Objective morality is not just about the bad things other people do. It affects us personally as well. We feel good when we do good, and we feel wrong when we do wrong. I've noticed that most people live each day loaded with a sense of guilt for the wrong things they have done in their lives. They live with this nagging sense that they have not measured up to a standard that is somehow being held over them. Why the guilty feeling? I believe that guilt is further evidence that objective moral values and duties exist.

Furthermore, we may only privately feel the folly of our own failures, but we certainly seem to enjoy publicly pointing out the failings of others. Have you noticed the pleasure the average person feels when they can condemn the behaviour of another? We are constantly pointing our fingers at the wrongs of *those* religious people" or "*those* liberals" or "*those* capitalists" or "*those* perverts."

The problem is, without any objective moral values and duties, we have no intellectual integrity to call the behaviour of others "right" or "wrong." This is how C.S. Lewis realized that the critic inside of him could not operate without a divine foundation of morality.

As an atheist, Lewis wanted to call the bad things he observed in the world "evil" and "unjust." He especially wanted to be critical of God and the evils he saw in the church. His problem came when he realized that, according to his atheistic worldview, he did not have the logical foundation to do so. Lewis realized he needed the God he was rejecting, to be able to call God, "unjust"! Read carefully why Lewis abandoned atheism, linking his need for God with his desire for justice:

> My argument against God was that the universe seemed to be cruel and unjust. But how had I got this idea of 'just' and 'unjust'?... What was I comparing this universe with when I called it 'unjust'?... Of course I could have given up my idea of justice by saying it was nothing but a private idea of my own. But if I did that, then my argument against God collapsed, too — for my argument depended on saying that the world was really unjust, not simply that it did not happen to please my private fancies... Consequently, atheism turns out to be too simple.[64]

Lewis wanted objective morality but could not find it in his atheistic worldview. He did the right thing and rather than pretend that objective morality existed apart from God, he converted to theism, a worldview that could support what he knew was true. To me, this looks like premise two is confirmed: Objective moral values and duties do exist. The conclusion is all that follows: *Therefore, God exists.*

WHAT IS GOD'S MORALITY LIKE?

The last three chapters have talked a great deal about the plausibility of the existence of God but have done little to show

---

[64] C.S. Lewis. *Mere Christianity.* (New York, NY.: MacMillan Publishers, 1960) p31.

what God is actually like. Many people reject God, not based on intellectual arguments, but because they do not like his character and how he runs the world. It is time to consider what kind of God could be behind this morality we observe in the world.

The Euthyphro Dilemma

Euthyphro was a character created by Plato who asked the tough question: *"Is something good because God wills it, or does God will something because it is good?"* Euthyphro wondered if there could be an instance where God could command that hating people is good. If that were the case, we could say that (since God commands it), hating is "good." Or, perhaps, is it always wrong to hate someone regardless of what God says about it?

This is a tough question, so tough it has been called *The Euthyphro Dilemma*. We must be careful how we answer this one. If we say that *all* God says, regardless of what he says, is *always* good, that could mean morality can change and is therefore, not objective. On this answer if God commanded us to hate, hating would now be considered good (because God said it).

If, on the other hand, we say that hating is *always* bad, independent of God's commanding it either way, we acknowledge that there *could* exist a morality apart from God. This would have atheist's ready to pounce on the violation of premise one, that if God does not exist, objective moral values and duties do not exist. This is a tricky dilemma.

Thankfully, the Euthyphro dilemma is easily solved once you look at the character of the Christian God. The dilemma becomes a false dichotomy presented by Plato (who only knew the rather human characteristics of the Greek gods and not Jesus Christ). In Christianity, there exists a third alternative: God wills good things because he himself is wholly good. Dr. Craig explains, "God's own nature is the standard of goodness, and his commandments to us are expressions of his nature."[65] God is the most loving, fair, compassionate, tender, strong, merciful, gracious and wonderful being imaginable. God would never command anything that would not end with the greatest amount of goodness to come as a result of anything he does or wills. Asking God to do anything outside of being good would be the same as asking a circle to be a square.

CONCLUSION

Even more than the previous two chapters, this chapter hits us right where we are. Each of us wakes up every day and has to answer the question of whether morality is something worth pursuing or not. Is it worthwhile to go to work? Is working hard a good idea or a bad idea? Should I choose to do what is right and noble today?

From a philosophical perspective, if God does not exist, I have tried to show why I believe there is no foundation for objective moral values and duties. Morality is then left to the preference of a person, a group of people, a government, a culture, or whatever. If this is the case, then we have little right to criticize any vicious culture or condemn any horrific act of violence as absolutely wrong.

Thankfully, objective moral values do exist. We have set up our communities and countries accordingly. The logic follows that if there are objective moral values and duties, they must come from a moral value and duty Giver.

Like C.S. Lewis, we must come to terms with the fact that God is the best explanation for why these objective moral values and duties exist. We can conclude like Lewis (in agreement with Premise Three): *Therefore, God exists.*

---

[65] William Lane Craig. *On Guard* (Grand Rapids, Mich.: Zondervan, 2010). p.136.

APPLICATION BREAK:
THE DIFFERENCE GOD MAKES

I once attended a lecture at the *University of British Columbia* where Dr. William Lane Craig was speaking on the evidence for God in light of a finely-tuned universe. Following the lecture, an undergraduate student asked a question during the Q and A time that I will always remember. She asked Dr. Craig,

"If we concede that there is a Designer who made the world, does that mean we should change the way that we are living?"

How would you answer that question? If there is a Designer, does that mean our lives should be lived differently? I believe that the existence of a Designer does actually change everything.

The good news is, that if there is a Designer, that means you are designed. It means that you were made for a purpose. How many people stumble through life wondering what their purpose is? You can start discovering what you were made for by learning about who made you.

The Bible says that you are God's masterpiece (Eph. 2:10, *NLT*). He has a plan for this world and has made you a part of it. Read the Bible and it is clear that the God of the universe knows who you are and wants you to know him personally.

He promises to care for you. He is bigger than your worries. That deep desire you have which you do not tell anyone about? He knows about it. That nagging fear that follows you around like a raincloud? He's bigger than that, too.

Think about it. Before the creation of the world, before anything or anyone existed, there was a living, loving God. There is not chaos at the centre. There is a Father.

The emptiness our earthly fathers have left in us should not be a deterrent from God but rather an invitation to have our needs fulfilled by him in the deepest part of our being.[66]

Should knowing all this change the way you live? I believe it should. Believing in God makes all the difference.

The following chapters will explore what God is like as he reveals himself in the story of the Bible and why you can trust it is actually His-story.

---

[66] Glenn T. Stanton. "Fatherhood: The Core of the Universe" Gospel Coalition Blog._www.thegospelcoalition.org/blogs/tgc/2012/06/14/fatherhood-the-core-of-the-universe. Accessed June 15, 2012.

THE BIBLE:
WHY WE CAN TRUST
WHAT GOD SAYS

"The Bible: Simple enough that a child can understand it; deep enough that a scholar can drown in it."

-Unknown

"You don't really believe all those things really happened, do you, Jon?" The question startled me, coming from my line-mate, Pete, while we sat on the bench catching our breath following a hard shift on the ice,

"After all," he added. "The Bible is just a bunch of ancient myths."

Pete and I had just met that first night of training camp for the Oxford Blues Ice Hockey team. I sat beside him sipping a water bottle and wondered how I would reply to his question before our next shift. Before that moment I had never had an apologetics discussion in the middle of a hockey game, nor was I trained to do so. I handed him the water bottle and explained, over the course of the hockey season, why I still trusted the Bible to be not just a collection of myths, but the actual truth. Let me share some of the highlights of this lengthy discussion.

HAS GOD REALLY SPOKEN?

If there is a God, we need his help in order to find out what he is like. Being of a totally different essence, God is too big for our human faculties to take in all at once. Thankfully, God comes to our level and speaks in a way we can understand.

The Bible declares that God is a communicator:

> "By the word of the Lord the heavens were made...Let all the earth fear the Lord; let all the inhabitants of the world stand in awe of him! *For he spoke, and it came to be*; he commanded, and it stood firm" (Psalm 33:6, 8-9. *Italics mine*).

Communication through revelation is part of what makes Christianity unique. It takes you from a vague idea of "there is some kind of something up there," to a personal God who communicates with us, revealing what he is like and how to have a relationship with him. Anything that could get in the way of that revelation would be disastrous to us either knowing about God or knowing him personally.

In Genesis 3 God's enemy, popularly known as "Satan", is introduced to us in the form of a serpent. In this passage, Satan is in the early days of recruiting humans to be part of the rebellion that he is leading against God. In these early days of humanity's existence, Satan asks them a very loaded question. It starts with four powerful words:

"Did God really say...?" (Gen. 3:1).

The serpent's objective is clear. He seeks to drive a wedge of doubt into Adam and Eve's confidence in what God has told them. Satan knows the power of undermining a human being's confidence in what God has revealed. Sadly, the serpent's temptation was successful. Adam and Eve second-guessed God's trustworthiness and then rejected his command. They sinned and ate the forbidden fruit. This was the beginning of the fallen world we all experience. All generations following would have a natural bent for rebelling against God and being skeptical or indifferent to what he has said. To this day, Satan's objective has not changed. Though his questions look a little different at times, they all contain the same idea:

- "Did God really all say those things actually happened?"
- "Did God really say that sex has to wait until you are married?"
- "Did God really mean only one man and one woman committed together for life?"
- "Did God really say that still applies to you today?"

When looking for examples of antagonism toward the Bible, one can easily find them in the pages of history, at a university, in the media or perhaps even in your own family. Friedrich Nietzsche, the nineteenth century German philosopher we met in chapter two, was never a big fan of Christianity, its influence in culture, or the sacred book upon which it relied. Nietzsche warned his readers:

> One does well to put on gloves when reading the New Testament; the proximity of so much impurity almost compels us to this...I have searched in it vainly for even a single congenial trait...everything in it is cowardice and self-deception.[67]

---

[67] Quote taken from Walter Kaufmann's biography, *Nietzsche: Philosopher, Psychologist, Antichrist* (Princeton, NJ.: Princeton University Press, 4th Edition, 1974) p378.

Many years later, a popular atheist writer named Christopher Hitchens (1944-2011) gained a following with his own public tirade against the Bible. Hitchens was very bold about his disapproval of the Bible and wanted his readers to know why they should not trust those who wrote it:

> The Bible may, indeed does, contain a warrant for trafficking in humans, for ethnic cleansing, for slavery, for bride-price, and for indiscriminate massacre, but we are not bound by any of it because it was put together by crude, uncultured human mammals.[68]

The effort by these men and others to undermine the message of the Bible has been going on generation after generation. The fact that the Bible has stood against all these attacks has inspired this poem and cartoon.[69]

THE SWORD THAT STOOD

Last night I passed by a swordsmith's door,

Startled by a piercing chime.

---

[68] Christopher Hitchens. *God Is Not Great: How Religion Poisons Everything*. (New York, NY.: Hachete Book Group, 2008). p143.

[69] This poem was inspired by a poem from John Clifford.

I saw there scattered on the floor,
Old hammers worn with time.
So many hammers, broken, now they lay.
"How many swords?" asked I.
"To break these tools in such a way?"

He smiled and gave this reply:
These hammers can split up every sort,
But this one sword won't take.
Try to distort they just can't thwart.
This sword they'll never break.

They pound and scream and cry and ring.
Hammers of all size and renown.

Neither size of king nor strength of swing
Can bring the strong sword down.

And so I thought just like God's Word

The skeptics beat upon.

The Word unharmed, be not alarmed

The sword has always won.

THE END

How has the Bible, this *sword that stood*, endured many years of opposition from its many critics?

I want to show why you can trust the process through which it was written, the care with which it was passed along, and the authority which it claims to have over our lives.

TRUST THE PROCESS

It is common for people to dismiss the Bible for one or all of three reasons: One, they think it is too old to be relevant; two, that it has been changed over time; or three, that it is full of contradictions. I want to show how all three criticisms are mistaken.

Timeless Truths Never Age

Is the Bible irrelevant simply because it is old? Parents understand the arrogance of a teenager dismissing their parent's opinion simply because they are "old." Sure, a parent's choice of clothing may no longer fit the trends of the past twenty years, but does truth ever trend, like wearing socks with sandals? We might ask: Have the laws of physics evolved this way? (Was there ever a time when it was OK to wear socks and sandals?) Could gravity ever go out of style and lose its relevance to us? Is there an era of history where "two plus two" has not equalled "four"? Of course not. Trends may come and go, but truth is timeless. The Bible is an ancient document, but dismissing it because of its age is not a valid reason to discredit the content within its pages. You may find that the Bible offers a perspective that the media or your friends, parents and teachers may overlook. Taking a look at what the Bible says could offer a perspective that you would never have seen within your own culture.

If truth does not change, perhaps as some have argued, the Bible's content has changed. If it has been changed, we would never know which parts are from God and what parts are either human error or a deliberate altering of the text. If such changes happened, the Bible would be untrustworthy as a document from God. Thankfully, we can test whether or not this is true by examining the process through which the Bible was passed down to us.

The Bible Came from God, Through Men, Throughout History

Let's look at the origin of the Bible. It is a process which many Christians have no idea about. This is why, when a new book or documentary is published saying that the Bible has been changed, many people believe the lies. Sadly, they do not know the truth. Here's how we got the Bible we read today.

1. *From God to the Old Testament Writers*

The Old Testament (OT) writers believed they were writing the words of God. Remember that if we were to know anything about God, it would have to be because God revealed it to us first. Moses, the ascribed writer of the first five books of the Bible, claims that is exactly what happened. Moses claimed to have penned his words as a revelation from God (Deut. 31:24–26). The claim of divine inspiration recurs throughout the OT in the works of other writers. We are told that Joshua wrote his words into the "book of the law of God" (Jos. 24:26). God told

Isaiah and Jeremiah to write what they had heard on tablets (Is. 30:8, Jer. 30:2). Put plainly, the OT claims to be the account of God speaking and revealing himself to humans for the benefit of others. In the New Testament (NT), Peter, references these OT prophets, "For no prophecy was ever produced by the will of man, but men spoke from God as they were carried along by the Holy Spirit" (2 Pet. 1:21). Here we see that the origin of our earliest Scriptures is not from the opinions of men but the very words of God.

2. *From the Old Testament Writers to Jesus and the Apostles*

Jesus quoted from the OT twenty-four times. In one such case, he confirmed the OT assertion that Moses was the one behind the first five books of the Bible. Jesus asked the Pharisees, "Have you not read in the book of Moses, in the passage about the bush, how God spoke to him...?" (Mark 12:26). The NT clearly affirms the divine inspiration of the OT. Paul confirms this when he instructs his disciple Timothy, "All Scripture is God-breathed" (2 Tim. 3:16).

Before he was crucified, Jesus told his disciples that more revelation would follow. He informed them that, after he returned to heaven, he would send the Holy Spirit as their teacher. "But the Counsellor, the Holy Spirit, whom the Father will send in my name, he will teach you all things, and bring to your remembrance all I have said to you" (John 14:26). The promised Holy Spirit would empower the disciples to be able to effectively receive God's revelation and then pass on the truth of the gospel as well as how to live as a Christian (both verbally and in writing).

The process by which God spoke to the writers of the Bible is what we call "inspiration." The books of the Bible were written as a partnership between God's inspiration and human design, human forms of argument, and the writer's preferred composition style. This becomes evident when you compare and contrast the various gospels with, for example, the writings of Paul.

Skeptics assert that the gospels were written long after Jesus had walked the earth. If that is true, they can disregard Jesus' claims of divinity, the miracles he performed and the first disciples' claim that he rose again after he was crucified. These extraordinary events are myths that would have developed over time, invented to bolster the divine authority of the early Christian movement. This accusation is a popular one with modern skeptics. We can discredit the argument by looking at what biblical scholarship tells us about the time between Jesus' life and when the gospels were written.

On a Saturday morning at Oxford's Wycliffe Hall, I woke up just in time for the last serving of breakfast. With the rest of the students either having already eaten or sleeping in, in an empty dining hall I ended up making conversation with an elderly man whom I had never before seen around the hall. I introduced myself and soon found out that my new breakfast buddy was actually a "celebrity."[70] Dr. Ken Bailey, an American-born Bible scholar, taught as a university professor in the Middle East for sixty years of his life. During his lifetime, he has become a leading, often quoted, expert in first century Middle Eastern culture. He is also a persistent defender of the trustworthiness of the Bible.

During our conversation over breakfast, Dr. Bailey pointed out how important memory is in Middle Eastern culture and community life. Everyone is expected to memorize the culture's sacred proverbs, poetry and scriptures. Dr. Bailey told me of a game played by kids in the Middle East that encourages this. Kids sit in a circle and one person starts by reciting a couple lines of a well known poem. The next person must pick up where the

---

[70] There are many who think that the words "celebrity" and "Bible-scholar" should never go together. I would agree with them...except for in the case of Dr. Ken Bailey who really is a celebrity Bible scholar.

other left off and continue with the passage. Any mistake results in the person who forgot his lines getting kicked out of the circle. Since everyone knows the piece so well, any hiccup in the recitation is caught immediately.

We can assume that the first-century apostles valued the accurate transmission of Jesus' words just as much as the children in this game do. Dr. Lindsay Arthur illustrates with a story of when missionary youth leaders tried to introduce the North American game "Telephone" to the Middle East. It failed to catch on.[71] Why was this? "Telephone" quickly loses its amusement when the message is always translated precisely. The kids do not see any fun in the game because they are culturally trained to repeat exactly what they hear.[72]

It is hard to get around the obvious fact that the NT writers believed the event they reported actually happened. As a service (and not to make a quick dollar), they took the time to pass the history on for future readers. Let's take a closer look at Luke, the writer of the gospel that bears his name.

Luke was a doctor who had a passion for research. Just like many of us today, Luke wanted to know what was true about Jesus. Listen to how he starts his gospel, writing to a man named Theophilus:

> Therefore, since I myself have carefully investigated everything from the beginning, it seemed good to me to write an orderly account for you, most excellent

---

[71] This is the game where one person whispers a message into the next person's ear. They have to pass on what they have heard to the next person. At the end of the line, the original message is so distorted that those playing usually deem this, "amusing."

[72] Arthur W. Lindsay "Can The Gospels Be Trusted?" From *Knowing And Doing* (Summer 2012 Edition) www.cslewisinstitute.org/ Can_The_Gospels_Be_Trusted_FullArticle. Accessed June 15, 2012.

> Theophilus, *so that you may know the certainty of the things you have been taught* (Luke 1:3, *italics mine*).

For those of us equipped with radars built to detect and reject a hidden sales pitch, Luke is a breath of fresh air. Luke immediately put his cards on the table, admitting his bias for writing. He wanted his readers to know that he was giving a thorough report of his research so that others could come to the same conclusions about Jesus as he had.

There are other reasons to trust Luke as a writer. Acts, another book he wrote, has been confirmed to be accurate in regard to all historical places and figures it describes. In fact, there are at least eighty-four historical facts that Luke got right. For example, he reports accurately the cultural practices of certain areas, the way the wind blows in certain places of the Mediterranean, and the depth of water in different harbours. Luke also identifies significant historical characters by name and title.[73]

3. *From the Apostles to the Early Church*

Once written, the gospel accounts were received by the early church and read aloud in their weekly gatherings.[74] The gospels were added to the OT text as inspired documents valued by the early church.

In the first century, the apostle Paul wrote a large portion of the NT primarily as letters to various churches he had started. At the

---

[73] Ie. Annas the high priest is mentioned in Acts 4:6 and 23:2, Ananias in 23:2, Herod Agrippa II in 12:1-3, 20, 23, Herod Agrippa II (25:13-26:32), Sergius Paulus in 13:7, Felix, the governor (23:23-24:27) and Festus (24:27). All these characters can be historically identified. For more see Driscoll and Breshears. (2010, p45).

[74] We know they met regularly because of the testimony of Acts 2:42, an ancient 2nd century manuscript called the *Didache* and a letter from Pliny The Younger, a Roman officer. These can be found at www.earlychristianwritings.com

end of his letter to the Colossians, Paul writes, "And when this letter has been read among you, have it also read in the church of the Laodiceans; and see that you also read the letter from Laodicea" (Col. 4:16). Letters from apostles such as Paul, Peter, or John were considered authoritative. Such writings were carefully duplicated and then passed around the Christian communities.

As the early church was persecuted, these letters became highly valued. While the Christians were running for their lives, we can assume that some of the texts they copied would have had slight variations. Though none of the textual variants are major, I have a great deal of sympathy for anyone who, while looking over his shoulder for those who are seeking to kill him, misprints a letter or two.

Scholarship reveals no major variation from the Bible they read to the one you now read. You will note that all throughout your Bible there are footnotes acknowledging where one (or more) recovered manuscript(s) gave a slightly different rendering of a word or phrase. Since there have been so many manuscripts discovered from antiquity, each finding makes it easier for scholars to note where a particular scribe added or omitted something.[75] Scholars point this out and footnote it in our modern Bibles. They do this to clearly acknowledge that no variances are being covered up or ignored.

Archaeology has revealed none of the original autographs of any text. Such a find would be next to impossible to find and then determine it was the original. What we do currently possess is approximately 14,000 copies of early versions of the NT. This is amazing considering that they were written on fragile parchments such as papyrus which were never stored with the intention of having them around for centuries. As the church grew, more copies were made and passed around. In light of

---

[75] This is done particularly well in the recent translation of the Bible, the *English Standard Version* (ESV).

heresies that emerged and spread, the early church fought hard to preserve the orthodox teaching of their authoritative Scriptures. Eventually all these authoritative texts were assembled together into one official book.

4. *From the Church to the Final List of Accepted Books*

A book or letter had to contain three key criteria in order to be accepted as authoritative and to be incorporated into the Bible. First, it had to be written by an apostle or a close associate of an apostle. Secondly, it could not contradict any other teaching in Scripture. Thirdly, it had to have widespread acceptance in the Christian community.[76]

Liberals and skeptics often point out other accounts of Jesus, such as the Gospels of Thomas, Judas or Mary. Just as we feel sorry for Cinderella who was left at home while her step-sisters all went to the ball, critics highlight these other gospels as forgotten yet just as worthy accounts of the life of Jesus. However disappointing to the arguments of contemporary scholars, the early church did not think they should be included in the Bible, as they did not fulfill the above three criteria.

Scholarship shows that the "Gnostic Gospels" (Thomas, Judas, Peter or Mary) were written later (some, much later) than the first century when Jesus walked. They contained strange, contradictory teachings that were not accepted by the early church.

The gospels and letters that did fit the three criteria were honoured as coming from God, through the apostles, and were then passed along to various Christian communities.

---

[76] Craig L. Blomberg, "Jesus of Nazareth: How Historians Can Know Him and Why It Matters" (Deerfield, IL: Christ on Campus Initiative, 2008), www.tgc-documents.s3.amazonaws.com/cci/Blomberg.pdf, p25–26.

It was not until the fourth century that a clear and definitive decision was made on what books were to be included in the completed Bible. Athanasius, an influential Christian leader, wrote a letter containing an exact list of the 27 books that make up our present day New Testament. Shortly after this letter was penned, a church council was held in Hippo in 393 AD and another in Carthage in 397 AD. It was here that Western churches officially agreed on which books would make up the Bible. [77] Did these meetings do anything to tinker with the books of the Bible? Was there a power struggle involved as so many critics have claimed?

Biblical scholar F.F. Bruce refutes this quite easily. Regarding the decisions made at these very formative church councils he states:

> One thing must be emphatically stated. The New Testament books did not become authoritative for the Church because they were formally included in a canonical list; on the contrary, *the Church included them in her canon because she already regarded them as divinely inspired*, recognizing their innate worth and generally apostolic authority, direct or indirect (*italics mine*).[78]

In case you are still curious about whether the Bible has been changed or not, you must know about a remarkable discovery made in the mountains of Qumran, Israel.

A Momentous Discovery

One day, in the middle of the late 1940s, an Arab boy was playing around some caves in Israel. Throwing a rock into one cave, he was surprised to hear what sounded to be the "clink" of

---

[77] Chris Price and Jon Morrison. *Questions*. (Vancouver, B.C.: Campus Fire Publishing, 2010).

[78] F.F. Bruce. *The New Testament Documents, Are They Reliable?* (Downers Grove, Ill.: InterVarsity Press, 1991). p 22.

some pottery. The curious sound led to the discovery of a treasure left by an ancient community. Hidden inside hundreds of clay pots were the historic documents we now call the *Dead Sea Scrolls*. These preserved manuscripts gave us copies of the Old Testament that were a thousand years older than any previous discovery. The study of these scrolls revealed that (with the exception of a word or two), our current texts were identical - nothing had been changed! Our trust in the Bible grew as it continues to do today as more discoveries are made.

Guilty Until Discovered Innocent

You do not always hear the stories of modern archaeology confirming biblical stories and places. They do not always make the evening news or paper. There are some very interesting finds in the field of biblical archaeology.

Before the twentieth century, the *Encyclopedia Britannica* considered the Hittites, a group of people mentioned in the Bible, a mythological civilization.[79] This was because the Bible was the only historical document that ever mentioned them. Archaeologists in modern Turkey eventually discovered evidence of Hittite culture, and now the famous encyclopedia will not only tell of the Hittites' existence, but it provides a detailed description of their civilization.[80]

Dr. John Elder offers this lengthy summary of such discoveries:

Little by little, one city after another, one civilization after another, one culture after another, whose memories were enshrined only in the Bible, were restored to their proper

[79] John Rogerson. *Old Testament Criticism in the Nineteenth Century: England and Germany* (London, UK.: SPCK, 1984).

[80] Credit to a L'Abri lecture from Francis Schaeffer called, "Five Problems With Those Who Deny the Claims of the Bible Concerning Itself" (Huemoz, Switzerland: L'Abri Tapes)

places in ancient history by the studies of archaeologists... *Nowhere has archaeological discovery refuted the Bible as history. (italics mine)*[81]

Archaeological discoveries continue to humble liberal scholars, exposing their *a priori* commitment to undermining the Bible's authority. The Bible proves to be a helpful tool for doing history when working alongside a trowel. According to Dr. Joseph P. Free, "We do not know of any cases where the Bible has been proved wrong."[82]

WHAT TO DO WITH TOUGH TEXTS

Admittedly, there are some passages in the Bible that are difficult to understand. Texts that are difficult to understand may undermine our confidence in the coherency of the Bible. With the help of some tools and the discipline to actually study what the text is saying, many difficult passages are explainable and worth the effort you put in to finding out what it is saying.

Dr. Wayne Grudem has footnoted in *Systematic Theology* when dealing with "Problem Texts," this reassurance, "In every one of those cases, upon close inspection of the text a plausible solution has become evident."[83]

Sometimes, finding that solution takes work. The reader has to roll up his sleeves and do some hard work. When I come across a difficult text, I first read through the whole context, paying attention to how this piece of Scripture relates to the whole of the Bible. For help with this, I fully endorse the *ESV Study Bible.*

---

[81] John Elder. *Prophets, Idols and Diggers* (New York, NY.: Bobbs Merrill, 1960), p. 16.

[82] Joseph P. Free *Archaeology and Bible History.* (Wheaton, IL.: Scripture Press, 1969) p. 1

[83] Wayne Grudem. *Systematic Theology.* (Grand Rapids, Michigan: Zondervan, 2000) Chapter 4 Footnotes.

Having a good Bible commentary written by a trusted Christian scholar can be helpful. Such a resource will provide background and insight into how a tough passage has been interpreted by trustworthy biblical scholars. Remember that we are not the first generation to read the Bible and wrestle with what it says![84]

Many times the truth emerges from a more careful reading of the English text, but other times it takes getting into the original Hebrew or Greek to find out what the text is saying. If you have not taken Greek or Hebrew, a good commentary will help with this.

By reading the seemingly tough passages within their context; with the help of a good study Bible and commentary; and by standing on the shoulders of conservative, trustworthy scholars, you too can see that the Psalmist was correct when he wrote, "The sum of your word is truth; and every one of your righteous ordinances endures forever (Ps. 119:160).

WHAT TO DO WHEN THE BIBLE OFFENDS YOU

For many people, it's not the process by which the Bible was passed down that upsets them; it is the content that they find most troubling.

As a pastor, I have had numerous conversations with people who found it tough to accept everything Christianity teaches. Many of these teachings are difficult to talk about, especially when it comes to religion, politics, economics or sexual ethics. That covers pretty much every awkward topic there is.

---

[84] Wayne Grudem recommends the following: Gleason L. Archer, *Encyclopedia of Bible Difficulties* (Grand Rapids: Zondervan, 1982); William Arndt, *Does the Bible Contradict Itself?* (St. Louis: Concordia, 1955); idem., Bible Difficulties (St. Louis: Concordia, 1932); and John W. Haley, *Alleged Discrepancies of the Bible* (1874; reprinted Grand Rapids: Baker, 1977).

The difficulty lies in the fact that the Bible will often take a position on an issue that goes directly against what people have learned in school, the media, from friends, or their parents. As a result, those I talk to are offended that the Bible would go against something that "everyone else" seems to think is okay.

What do *you* do when the Bible says something offensive to you?

Dr. Timothy Keller, a pastor from New York, offers some insight into why the Bible sometimes conflicts with our culture. In his *New York Times* bestselling book, *The Reason for God*,[85] Keller acknowledges that offensive texts actually argue in favour of the Bible's credibility. Counter-cultural teachings serve to show us that the Bible could be true and transcendent after all.

If there were a system of belief set up whereby you agreed with everything it ever taught, it is likely that someone who shared your culture and values had just made it up. If there were a divine being that agreed with everything you ever thought or did, it would be more likely that you made a god in your image rather than God making you in his.

When the Bible offends you, be encouraged that it offends everyone at some point. Consider the responsibility of the Bible. It must speak the truth to every culture through every era of history. I believe that there has never been a culture on earth that has not been offended by the Bible on some issue. What offends one group could be common sense to another and vice versa. Some cultures are offended that God would judge people for their sin. Some cry out to God to judge people because of sin. There are some cultures that are appalled at how God would forgive people no matter what they have done. For other cultures, that kind of forgiveness is expected of God.

In his famous sermon, *The Weight of Glory,* C.S. Lewis taught how it is the challenging parts of the Bible that we must consider

---

[85] Tim Keller. *The Reason For God.* (Penguin Group, 2008). p113.

most seriously. For example, the doctrine of the Trinity, the belief that God is three persons and yet also still one being, is a core, Christian belief. Central as it may be, the idea of three-and-yet-one is difficult for us to fathom. If the Trinity were easy to understand, I would be concerned that we humans made it up. Therefore, Lewis would argue that these kind of difficult truths serve as evidence for a transcendent origin to Christianity. According to Lewis:

> If our religion is something objective, then we must never avert our eyes from those elements in it which seem puzzling or repellent; for it will be precisely the puzzling or the repellent which conceals what we do not yet know and need to know.[86]

God wants to communicate with us. He wants to help us live the life for which he has created us. He does this because he loves us. God lovingly reveals truth to us and how we are to live in light of that truth. Even though we may not understand everything, when we trust the Bible, we are trusting that God knows what is best.

CONCLUSION

If my line-mate Peter was right about the Bible being a bunch of myths, there would be little reason to believe that it could be trustworthy to tell us anything about God or serve as an authority to govern our lives. It really comes down to one question:

Can we trust that the Bible is actually what God has said to us?

We should be concerned that Satan was the one who originally asked this question and that the response was historically devastating. Having been so successful in one generation after

---

[86] C.S. Lewis. "The Weight Of Glory." Preached originally as a sermon in the *Church of St Mary the Virgin* in Oxford, England on June 8, 1942.

another, Satan has not stopped asking this question. If you are ever questioned about the reliability of the Bible, you can remember these four points:

1. *The Bible is authentic.* It comes to us from God who spoke through his Holy Spirit to the writers of the Old and New Testaments.

2. *The Bible is trustworthy.* The Bible's message is consistent - it's about God's plan of saving people as revealed through Jesus.

3. *The Bible's contents are unchanging.* This book has been faithfully preserved throughout history.

4. *The Bible is authoritative.* If God has spoken in the Bible, and if God is good, we should be able to trust what he says. Since God is all-knowing, he has access to information that transcends all time and every culture. When we disagree with something the Bible says, we can be sure that we are the ones with the limited information. We can learn to trust the Bible's teachings and then submit to what it says.

Those are four good reasons to counter the four deadly words, "Has God really said...?" My hope is that you can now see that the best response to the question has always been, "Yes, he has."

THIS IS JESUS:
THE MAN WHO WAS ALSO GOD

"Who is this? Even the wind and the waves obey him!"

-Matthew 4:41

"...the single most powerful figure–not merely in these two millennia but in all human history–has been Jesus of Nazareth."

-Time Magazine, December 6, 1999

Time Magazine considered Jesus Christ the most powerful figure in history. This is astounding, considering he lived a short life in a rural part of the Roman Empire.

To understand world history, you really need to have some understanding of what and who Jesus was all about. This chapter will help you sort that out.

THE TROUBLE WITH TRUTH AND LIES

This is the story of two friends: Truth (left) and Lies (right).

The following story details how their friendship fell apart.

One day Truth and Lies were having a lovely time at a private pool party.

Knowing that nobody was around, the boys decided to try skinny-dipping (swimming without their swim suits).

When Truth went underwater, Lies grabbed Truth's swim suit and all his clothes. Lies ran home before Truth surfaced.

Truth had a feeling that Lies had run home so he ran straight to his house.

He knocked on the door at Lies' house, and sure enough, there was his friend wearing all of Truth's clothes. Truth confronted Lies, but Lies denied the whole thing. He claimed he had been at home all day and that the clothes he was wearing were his own.

Truth was furious. He pulled his friend out into the street and demanded they fight about it.

The neighbours were absolutely appalled at what they saw. They called the police to break up the fight.

The policeman stepped in and pulled the two boys aside.

"What is going on here?" the cop asked.

"*I* will tell you what is going on," exclaimed Truth.

"We were swimming in a pool and decided to go skinny dipping. I went underwater, and Lies here took off with all my clothes and ran home! Now he is wearing all my clothes, and I want them back!"

"Is he correct?" asked the officer to Lies.

"No sir, he is not correct," Lies answered. "You see, I've been home all day watching TV. These are my clothes and I do not know where these accusations are coming from."

"Hmm..." puzzled the officer. It seemed he had a tough decision to make. He had two boys with two very different stories.

In the end, the officer had to figure out the same thing that we all need to figure out about Jesus...

Who should we believe: *Lies in Truth's clothing or the naked Truth?*

AN IMPRESSIVE RESUME

Though we do not know the exact date of his birth, history speaks of two eras; from all the days prior to his birth (BC) and all that has happened since (AD/CE). Though he was not an author, more books have been written about him than any other figure in history. The book in which he is the main character, the

119

Bible, is the best selling book of all time. It has been translated into over two thousand languages worldwide. Even today, Bible translators are hard at work ensuring that there is a Bible in every language spoken on the planet.

From what we know, Jesus never painted a picture, wrote a poem, or composed a piece of music. He has, however, inspired more works of art, literature, and music than any other leader or than all other philosopher. A film about Jesus' life has been reproduced in 100 different languages and has been viewed by more people than any other film in history. During his life, Jesus never left a small region in the Middle East and yet today his influence continues to grow in every country of the world. Jesus never led an army, but millions have laid down their lives for his cause. Historian Philip Schaff adds, "Jesus..., without money and arms, conquered more millions than Alexander, Caesar, Mohammed, and Napoleon...he shed more light on things human and divine than all philosophers and scholars combined..."[87]

Each week, Jesus is worshipped by people from all ethnicities, cultures, sub-cultures and social levels. Royalty and peasants alike honour Jesus as their leader. From Oxford to Darfur; Canada to India- the number of Jesus' followers grows daily. [88]

Despite his influence, history is still divided about what to do with Jesus. Nations are divided. Families are divided. I would imagine that some reading this right now are divided about how they should feel about Jesus.

---

[87] Taken from Josh McDowell's, *Evidence That Demands A Verdict*, (San Bernardino, Here's Life Publishers, 1972). Chapter 8.

[88] For help with this survey of Jesus' influence I am in debt to RZIM speaker, Tom Price, who used this material in a sermon at St. Aldates Church in Oxford. It was adapted from the 1926 essay by James Allen Francis called, "One Solitary Life".

Some people honour him while others mock him. Some say he was an astounding teacher and others that he was a dreadful deceiver. Public perspectives on Jesus and what he stood for are numerous and diverse.

Before we look at *who* he was, let's first establish *if* Jesus was.

THE HISTORICAL JESUS

Some extreme skeptics argue that the historical figure, Jesus Christ of Nazareth, was merely an idea, a mythological character invented by the early church. Some suggest that early church leaders borrowed the story of God coming as a man, dying for sin and rising again, from various Egyptian and Greek mythologies. Are they right? Have the masses been deceived? How can we know if Jesus actually existed?

Serious scholars (be they Christian or not) are unanimous that those denying Jesus' existence are seriously mistaken. The historic evidence that Jesus was indeed a real, historical figure is overwhelming. Dr. Craig Evans writes:

> No serious historian of any religious or nonreligious stripe doubts that Jesus of Nazareth really lived in the first century and was executed under the authority of Pontius Pilate, the governor of Judea and Samaria.[89]

There are several early historical accounts of Jesus life that come to us from outside of the Bible. Most prominent is the work of a Jewish historian employed by the Roman Empire named Josephus. Josephus specialized in writing about notable first-century Jewish affairs. No doubt Jesus would have caused enough of a stir in those days to get a mention in their annals.

---

[89] Craig Evans. *Jesus and His World: The Archaeological Evidence.* (Westminster, John Knox Press, 2012).

From Josephus (and echoed in the work of another writer named Tacitus) we learn that Jesus was crucified under a Roman governor named Pilate. We also learn from a writer named Mara bar Serapion that Jewish leaders were involved in the accusation and trial of Christ.

In *The Historical Jesus*, Gary Habermas concludes that we can safely call it a historical fact that Jesus existed, that he was crucified under a Roman governor named Pontius Pilate, that he was buried, and that his disciples claimed that he rose again from the dead.[90]

Perhaps my favourite quote in favour of the historical Jesus comes from the insightful UK based journalist, Matthew Parris. Parris, not a Christian himself, finds the person of Jesus so astounding that he could not have been made up. Parris writes:

> One of the reasons we can be pretty sure Jesus actually existed is that if He had not, the Church would never have invented Him. He stands so passionately, resolutely and inconveniently against everything an established church stands for. Continuity? Tradition? Christ had nothing to do with stability. He came to break up families, to smash routines, to cast aside the human superstructures, to teach abandonment of earthly concerns and a throwing of ourselves upon God's mercy. Jesus came to challenge precisely what today's unbelieving believers in belief so prize in what they presume to be faith.[91]

---

[90] Gary Habermas. *The Historical Jesus: Ancient Evidence For The Life Of Christ*. (College Press Publishing Company, 1996) See Chapter 9.

[91] Matthew Parris. "Beware – I Would Say To Believers – The Patronage Of Unbelievers. The Spectator. February 25, 2012. www.spectator.co.uk/columnists/matthew-parris/7667978/beware-i-would-say-to-believers-the-patronage-of-unbelievers/ Accessed February 12, 2013.

It is, therefore, intellectually responsible to say that Jesus of Nazareth really lived. What was it about him that was so notable? Let's look at a few attributes for which Jesus is best known.

THE TEACHER OF TEACHERS

One of the ways Jesus stood out was through his teaching. The NT gospels testify that Jesus could both draw and hold a crowd. Crowds would forsake meals just to follow him around all day and listen to his teaching. Jesus astounded the crowds to whom he spoke. They marvelled at what he said and left them wanting more. One time Jesus drew fifteen thousand people to hear him speak- that is some kind of teacher![92]

Jesus' teachings have influenced Christians and non-Christians alike. He was the one who gave us the Golden Rule, "Do to others as you would have them do to you" (Luke 6:31). He was the first leader to teach his followers that it is better to love one's enemies than to scorn them or kill them. Jesus taught that it is better to give than to receive[93], and he taught the well known stories of the Good Samaritan and the Prodigal Son.[94]

Though his public teaching lasted only three years, it has been scrutinized by scholars in every science—among them theology, philosophy, psychology, and sociology to name a few. Jesus' influence has founded universities like Oxford, Cambridge, Yale, Princeton, and Harvard. Now spanning the entire globe, Jesus'

---

[92] The miraculous "Feeding of the 5000" only included a count of the men present. There were likely more women than men in attendance (this always happens in church history) plus the children that would have been present. Fifteen thousand is the more likely number.

[93] Paul quotes Jesus' line in Acts 20:25

[94] If you do not know these stories, do a search of Luke 10:25-37 and Luke 15:11-32.

followers have been inspired throughout the centuries to set up educational institutions to teach what he taught.

Having followed Jesus for most of my life, I still marvel at his teaching and their relevance in my own life. Every time I read the gospels, I am challenged by what Jesus taught. His words challenge my own choices and expose my selfish, proud and sinful motives. They reveal my need for his leadership over my life. They tell me of my need for his grace. With each mistake I make, I realize that things would have gone better if I had simply obeyed what he said.

THE GOD OF THE UNIVERSE

Jesus was a great teacher, but he will not allow you to cap his credentials as simply that of a wise sage. Jesus also said he was God. What are we to make of that bit of teaching? C.S. Lewis warns us about patronizing or dismissing Jesus with simply his status as the "greatest moral teacher" or something like that:

> I am trying here to prevent anyone saying the really foolish thing that people often say about Him: "I'm ready to accept Jesus as a great moral teacher, but I don't accept His claim to be God." That is the one thing we must not say. A man who said the sort of things Jesus said would not be a great moral teacher. He would either be a lunatic — on a level with the man who says he is a poached egg — or else he would be the Devil of Hell. You must make your choice. Either this man was, and is, the Son of God: or else a madman or something worse. You can shut Him up for a fool, you can spit at Him and kill Him as a demon; or you can fall at His feet and call Him Lord and God. But let us not come with any patronizing nonsense about His being a great human teacher. He has not left that open to us. He did not intend to.[95]

---

[95] C.S. Lewis. *Mere Christianity* (New York, NY : HarperCollins, 1952). p52.

124

How can a respected Oxford academic like Lewis be so insistent about worshipping a human being as God?

It is helpful to know we are not the first ones to wonder whether an educated, civilized person can really believe God could ever become a human being.

In an effort to dismiss this decision, some have tried to argue that Jesus never claimed divinity. It is suggested that divinity was a status given to him by his early followers in an effort to boost his credentials.

According to Jesus, his divinity was a matter of fact. Though we do not have Jesus saying explicitly, "I am God", there are plenty of references to Jesus dropping this truth on his crowds. A Jewish person of that era believed God's name was too holy to speak. Instead, they used other words to refer to God. Jesus knew this and alluded to it in a manner appropriate for his first century audience.

- Jesus declared, "I AM," echoing God's self-identification to Moses in the OT book of Exodus (John 6:34, 6:48, 8:12, 8:58, 10:9, 10:11, 11:25, et al).
- Jesus said he existed before Abraham, the father of the Jewish people (John 8:58).
- Jesus claimed that he and God the Father were united as one (John 10:30).
- When the religious leaders accused Jesus of claiming to be God. Jesus never backed down or denied their allegations (Matt. 26:65).
- When Jesus was resurrected, his disciples worshipped him as God (Matt. 28:17).
- He said he had the authority to forgive sins (Luke 5:20).

Suggesting you have the authority to forgive sins is a preposterous assumption unless you are the one who was wronged. It would be strange for you to apologize to a friend for the time you stepped on my foot. The third party was not the one harmed— unless the friend is God, and therefore, all sins are sins against him (Ps. 51:4). This is why a statement such as Jesus made telling the paraplegic that his sins were forgiven was so shocking for people to hear.

Based on their reactions, they knew exactly what he was saying. Some wanted him killed for blasphemy. Some saw what he was doing and worshipped him. Jesus did not seem to have any problem with people exalting him in this way. I personally always appreciate kind words from my friends... but I never allow it to go as far as accepting their worship.

William Biederwolf draws from the evidence this very strong comparison: "A man who can read the New Testament and not see that Christ claims to be more than a man, can look all over the sky at high noon on a cloudless day and not see the sun."[96]

Is Jesus God or not? According to him he most certainly is. According to others, this claim was deserving of death. The Romans then killed him by a process called "crucifixion." Understanding Jesus' death in this way is crucial to understanding what he was all about.

THE SAVIOUR OF THE WORLD

There is nothing that's special about a poor, homeless, unmarried, Middle Eastern man being executed for crimes against the Roman Empire. Why then, when it happens to Jesus does it become such a big deal? Why, some two thousand years later, are people still talking about his death, singing about his death, writing about his death and wearing crosses around their necks to celebrate his death?

---

[96] Taken from Frank Mead. *The Encyclopedia of Religious Quotations* (Westwood, Ill.: Fleming H. Revell, n.d.), p. 50.

The gospels tell us that Jesus was taken by Roman soldiers to a place just outside of Jerusalem known as "The Skull." There he was crucified. We do not have many details about what crucifixion was like. What seems to be taken as commonplace by these first-century writers has become a foreign practice to us.

What it Could Be Like to Be Crucified

A cross was an instrument for killing criminals in the ancient world. Death by crucifixion was a horrific way to die. Crucifixion was initially practiced by the Persians and further adapted by the Romans.[97]

In a crucifixion, the condemned criminal was stripped naked and either nailed or bound by ropes to two wooden beams. John 20:25 tells that Jesus was crucified with nails that pierced his wrists and feet. Noteworthy, Isaiah the prophet foresaw this happening approximately seven hundred years beforehand when he says, "they will look on the one whom they have pierced" (Is. 53:5). Crucifixion was done in public so as to maximize humiliation and to serve as a crime-deterrent for others. Dr. Truman Davis gives us a sample of what Jesus would have experienced while hanging on the cross.

> As the arms fatigue, great waves of cramps sweep over the muscles, knotting them in deep, relentless, throbbing pain. With these cramps comes the inability to push himself upward. Hanging by his arms, the pectoral muscles are paralyzed, and the intercostal muscles are unable to act. Air can be drawn into the lungs, but cannot be exhaled. Jesus fights to raise himself in order to get even one short breath. Finally, carbon dioxide builds up in the lungs and in the bloodstream, and the cramps partially subside. Spasmodically, he is able to push himself upward to exhale and bring in the life-giving oxygen.

---

[97] Dr. Truman Davis is credited with the bulk of my understanding of crucifixion from a physician's perspective.

After a while, orthostatic collapse through insufficient blood circulating to the brain and heart would follow. The only way the victim could avoid this was to push up by his feet so the blood could be returned to some degree of circulation in the upper part of his body.[98]

For many years, people questioned the Bible's claim that Jesus was crucified with nails. The accusation was used as an example of why the Bible cannot be trusted as a historic document, that it was false and misleading. "The Use of Nails in the Crucifixion" was the leading article for such skepticism. Written by Dr. J. W. Hewitt, the *Harvard Theological Review* article reported there is, "astonishingly little evidence that the feet of a crucified person were ever pierced by nails."[99] Hewitt argued that nails through the feet would have ripped through flesh, thus making it unable to support a hanging body.

In June of 1968, new research revealed that Hewitt was mistaken. An archaeological discovery by Dr. Vassilios Tzaferis confirmed the use of nails in crucifixion. He discovered a tomb containing a body that had been pierced with seven inch spikes through the heels. Additionally, in correlation with the gospel account of the soldiers breaking the legs of the men crucified beside Jesus, the calf bones of the discovered skeleton were shattered.[100] The

---

[98] Truman Davis, "The Crucifixion of Jesus," quoted in *Expositor's Bible Commentary: Matthew, Mark Luke*. Volume 8.

[99] J.W. Hewitt. "The Use of Nails in the Crucifixion" *Harvard Theological Review*. 25:29-45.

[100] Often the calf bones of an individual were broken to accelerate death. The thieves crucified beside Jesus had theirs broken but since Jesus was already pronounced dead, the Roman soldiers did not break his calves. John's gospel (19:33) links this to the Messianic prophecies of Psalm 34:20 and Exodus. 12:46.

cause of death, according to Dr. N. Haas of Israel's *Hadassah Medical School*, was evident: "Crucifixion."[101]

On the day he was crucified, (having struggled immensely for breath) Jesus would have been exhausted. Amazingly, he still managed to dialogue with the thieves at his side and also with some friends and onlookers. With his last bit of energy, Jesus would have pushed up on the nails, taken a breath and then spoken his last words, "It is finished." John understates the Saviour's last moment with these words, "and he bowed his head and gave up his spirit" (John 19:30).

That day, on a wooden cross just outside of Jerusalem, the Son of God was declared dead.

Why Did Jesus Have to Die?

It can be tempting to read what happened and feel sorry for Jesus. This is an understandable reaction. After all, he was betrayed, abandoned, beaten, whipped, mocked, shamed and violently killed. Though empathy and compassion can be appropriate responses to this, we must never mistake Jesus for a victim. He was no victim. He was a willing substitute. Jesus was never forced to die on a cross. He willingly gave up his life for a purpose that he felt was worth the sacrifice. Jesus explains his own motivations for his death:

> No one takes it [my life] from me, but I lay it down of my own accord. I have authority to lay it down and I have authority to take it up again. This charge I have received from my Father (John 10:18).

The Bible makes the purpose of Jesus' death clear: Jesus died for sinners (Rom. 5:8). Paul reiterates this in his letter to the Corinthians, "Christ died for our sins" (1 Cor. 15:3).

---

[101] Josh McDowell. *Evidence For The Historical Jesus*. (Eugene, Or. Harvest House Publishers, 1993). p212.

Why did Jesus have to die for sin? Why could God not just forgive everyone without any of this violence or death? Death was a consequence of our choice to sin. In Genesis, God promised Adam and Eve that the consequence of their rebellion would be death. "If you eat of this fruit, you will surely die" (Genesis 2:17). Romans 6:23 states very clearly that "the wages of sin is death." When we sin, we earn death. That is what sinners deserve.

Rather than people paying the price for their sin, the good news is that, for those who receive his offer, Jesus becomes a willing substitute for them.

2 Corinthians 5:21 is an important commentary in understanding what else took place in that moment when Jesus died. The Apostle Paul tells us, "God made him who knew no sin to become sin for us so that in him we might become the righteousness of God" (2 Cor. 5:21).

Two things are said to be happening here. Firstly, our sin was nailed to Jesus' cross. He, took it as our substitute. The book of Colossians explains:

> You who were dead in your trespasses and the uncircumcision of your flesh, God made alive together with him, having forgiven us all our trespasses, by cancelling the record of debt that stood against us with its legal demands. This he set aside, nailing it to the cross (Col. 2:13-15).

The Father placed the wrath for sin upon the Son so that it would not have to be placed upon us. Secondly, not only does Jesus take our sin, we receive something important. Paul says, "that we might become the righteousness of God." This means we are given a clean, sinless slate. It is Jesus' perfect record given on our behalf. The result is that, in God's sight, Christians are declared "righteous." They are now "in right standing" before

God. With Jesus' perfect righteousness now given to us, Hebrews 4:16 assures us that we are able to come freely and confidently into the presence of God.

Jesus becomes the only access a sinner can have to God. Without him, there is simply no other way for anyone to approach a holy God. There is no back door, no side route and no other Saviour.

THE EXCLUSIVITY OF JESUS AND THE CONSIDERATION OF OTHER RELIGIONS

The exclusive claims of Christianity rub a lot of people the wrong way. In John 14:6, Jesus made what seems a most narrow-minded statement. His announcement to the world is enough to make a twenty-first century, Western pluralist's toenails curl. He declared, "I am the way, the truth and the life, *no one comes to the Father but through me*" (John 14:6, *italics mine*).

Jesus' words are slightly less shocking when you consider that exclusive claims to truth are more common than we know. Truth is, by its nature, exclusive. Two differing claims cannot both be right. Math teachers make exclusive claims all the time. They will tell you that the multiplication table is not up for negotiation. There are right answers and wrong ones. A doctor's prescription is an exclusive claim as well. It excludes every medication except the one that is written on the prescription paper. A person who gives you their phone number is telling you to exclude dialing all other numbers except the digits they have provided you.

Religious leaders make exclusive claims because they believe, that when it comes to God, there are things that are right and things that are wrong.

Who isn't making exclusive claims today?

Religious pluralism is a popular belief in Western culture. At first it sounds very inclusive, but it is really just as exclusive as any other claims. Religious pluralists are those who argue that the "real God" is actually a mix of the gods of *all* the religions combined (ie. the Christian, Jewish, Muslim, Hindu, Sikh, Jehovah's Witness; and we can even throw in ancient Greek gods). By mixing all the major religions, they are discounting the exclusive truth claims to which religions strictly adhere.

Do All Religions Lead to the Same God?

Understand that by trying to combine *all* religions like this, pluralists are just creating a *new* religion. They bring forth a *new* description of God with which none of the included religions would agree. In my experience talking with pluralists, I have found them to be extremely exclusive. That is, unless I *agree* with them, I am not generally accepted by them. Pluralists will accept you as long as you accept everything *they* believe. If you do not agree, do not expect to get invited to their parties. The fact that those who think they are most tolerant could actually be this intolerant is quite ironic.

All religions now considered, our choice becomes who we want to best identify with when we stand in judgment before God. Who will be your advocate before him? Would you choose Jesus, or do you want to try another? Would it be Mohammed, Confucius, Ghandi, Buddha, Karl Marx or some other historical figure? These all may have taught interesting things but I wonder how far their righteousness will get you. Could they pay the price of your sin? Not one of them claims to offer this. Alternatively, you could try to represent yourself before a holy God, but I'm not sure that conversation would last very long.

The Christian belief is that Jesus, as God, is the only one who can bring humanity back to God. He was the only person in history with such a pedigree. 1 Timothy 2:5 tells us plainly, "There is one God, and there is one mediator between God and men, the man Christ Jesus." As a man, he could represent humanity. He was tempted in every way, and yet he never sinned.[102] Jesus is our proverbial "best foot forward" as far as humanity goes. Jesus is also God. As such he is able to serve as a "middle man" and usher us into the very presence of God.

The amazing thing is that Jesus offers his righteousness to anyone who will receive it. Rather than being receptive to this offer, we complain there are not other ways to God. While it is incredibly gracious that God would offer *any way* back to him, people complain that he did not provide ten ways.

The offer for salvation is available to all. Instead of being exclusive, Christianity is actually very *inclusive*. Everyone is welcome to come to Jesus. It does not matter who they are, or what they have done. The Bible tells us, "...*whoever* believes in him shall have eternal life" (John 3:16). Whether they be Jew, Hindu, Sikh, Greek, Canadian, African, athlete, entrepreneur, lawyer, or academic, the offer is there — come to Jesus.

THE FRIEND OF SINNERS

Jesus made us to be in relationship with him. He made you because he loves you. Did you get that? Jesus loves you. It was love that motivated his death on the cross for each person, you included. It is his love that now calls you back to himself.

It always saddens me when people keep their distance from God because they think he is some sort of tyrant or prude. God is very warm and inviting. Jesus said, "No longer do I call you servants...but I have called you friends" (John 15:15). Jesus does not want us thinking of God as some slave-master and us as his slaves. He wants us to know him as friend. That's quite a difference. That's quite an offer.

Do not miss this attribute of Jesus. In light of what has already been said in this chapter, it is simply astounding that the God of

---

[102] Anselm, *Cur Deus Homo?* Book II, ch. 6.

133

the universe would call us his friend. As creator of the world, Jesus is bigger than the entire cosmos. He is also small enough to be with you wherever you are reading this. Jesus speaks, and the world is made. He also speaks to the needs of our hearts. Jesus holds the nations as a drop in a bucket. He also holds our lives in his hands. Jesus knows all things regarding the past, present and future. He even knows how many hairs you have on your head. (Luke 12:7). Jesus has a plan for world history (Heb. 1:3). He has a plan for your life as well (Jer. 29:11).

God calls me "friend." I can think of no greater foundation in my life than to know God and be known by him. He has never, and will never, leave me. He has been there collecting my tears in my most difficult days and has celebrated with me in my most triumphant joys. Though our relationship is unique compared to every other friend I have, I cherish this friendship more than anything else in the world.

Jesus is simply the greatest possible being I could ever imagine. He is to be known not only as Creator, Teacher, God and Saviour. - he wants us to know him as Friend.

WHAT ABOUT YOU? KNOWING JESUS PERSONALLY

This Jesus is a polarizing figure. People either crown him as Lord or kill him as a criminal. One thing we cannot do is land somewhere in the middle. His claims are too dramatic, his demands are too costly, his influence is too revolutionary.

In the middle of Luke 9, following one of his famous miracles, Jesus sat down for a rest with his disciples. Interested in what people were saying about him, Jesus asked, "Who do the crowds say that I am?" After collecting the answers, Jesus turned the question back on his disciples. "Who do you say that I am?" (Luke 9:20). This is when Jesus' questions start to get very personal.

There is a difference between knowing about someone and really knowing them. It is one thing to know a lot *about* your favourite athlete or musician. You can know all about their hometown, their family situation, their career statistics, and what their hobbies and interests are. It is another thing entirely to know someone personally.

I said I would help you understand what Jesus of Nazareth was all about. We know he existed. He has influenced culture with his life and teaching more than any other person in history. He claimed to be God. He died on a cross. He rose again three days later. He said he would give forgiveness of sin and eternal life to all who believe in him.

You can read all these things about Jesus but never actually know him.[103] You can know his titles, the miracles he performed, and all the things he taught. You may know what other people say about Jesus. His question to his disciples then still stands for us today:

"Who do *you* say that I am?"

---

[103] If you want to know Jesus personally, you can turn to the appendix of this book at any time. There are some instructions there that should help.

THE HELL CHAPTER:
HOW GOD IS LOVE BUT NOT ALL WILL BE SAVED

"Some will not be redeemed. There is no doctrine which I would more willingly remove from Christianity than this, if it lay in my power. But it has the full support of Scripture and, specially, of Our Lord's own words; it has always been held by Christendom; and it has the support of reason."

-C.S. Lewis, The Problem Of Pain.

What would we do in a world without justice? I think people would hate it.

Whenever I am traveling abroad, I am proud to tell people that I am from Canada. I love being from Canada. I love being from

Vancouver, too. Vancouver is consistently voted one of the nicest places in the world to live. Vancouverites are proud of that even though the rest of Canada hates us for it.

There is, however, one thing of which we Vancouver folk are not very proud. Around the world, people I meet are always keen to remind me about this stain on our proverbial "I Heart Vancouver" shirt (aka a Vancouver Canucks jersey). The conversation goes something like this:

People I Meet: "You're from Vancouver. You're the people who riot when your team loses a hockey game."

Me: (Staring blankly) "...Yup...I guess that's us."

The first riot happened in the spring of 1994. Just as some became convinced it was a freak, one-off, city-wide lapse of judgment, it happened again in the spring of 2011. I remember the riots of 2011 much better than 1994.

In 2011, the Vancouver Canucks came nail-bitingly close to winning their first Stanley Cup - the greatest prize in the hockey world. Canuck fans had been waiting forty years for their team to win the Cup. 2011 was destined to be our year. After four rounds of grueling playoff hockey, the Canucks took the Boston Bruins to a seventh and final game. The Canucks were one win away from winning the Stanley Cup!

On a sunny spring night in beautiful Vancouver, British Columbia, the entire city watched the game either live at Rogers Arena, around flat screens in their homes with friends, or on the streets of downtown Vancouver. The city of Vancouver hosted an enormous party, setting up huge screens so the public could gather and celebrate the historic occasion together.

Sadly, the history books tell us that on June 14, 2011, the Vancouver Canucks lost game seven. Instead of the Canucks, the Boston Bruins won the Stanley Cup that year. News reporters quickly shifted from the predictable shots of celebrating Bruins and crying Canucks to report that a riot had broken out in the streets. Cars were being flipped over and burned, designer stores had their windows smashed and were looted. Fights broke out all over as the city core went loco.

The city was in chaos. In some cities they riot to protest government oppression. In Vancouver, we riot because of lost hockey games.

Several hours later the riot police brought the city back to order. Millions of dollars were lost in the vandalism, theft and destruction. The city's reputation was internationally smeared because of what happened that night. Moving forward, I now have to explain the situation to every international that I meet.

In the aftermath of this debacle, Vancouverites were furious. The vast majority of people watched these events unfolding on their TV screens. Those caught rioting on camera were instantly vilified in all the media.

Vancouverites demanded that those who participated in the riots be caught, sentenced and punished severely. I figured that if there were public lynchings or hangings in contemporary Canadian jurisdiction, they would have been demanded as well! Not only in the media, but around water coolers all over the city, people talked about how important it was for "those who did this" to be punished. Across Canada, I witnessed an appeal to justice that I have never seen before from this otherwise laid back, "do what feels right" kind of city.

The police calmed the public by assuring them that the evidence was being sorted through and that justice would be served in the city. The public was calmed by this and waited as the police did their job sorting through the evidence and pursuing the offenders. As months passed, no arrests were made. The level of justice in the city, the province of British Columbia, and the nation of Canada became a popular topic of debate. People wondered whether they could trust a government that could not enforce its own laws. Would the guilty be let off the hook? Would justice be served in Canada?

I say that I had never seen this kind of reaction before because at that same time, a book aimed at questioning the historical, biblical position regarding God's attribute of justice became an overnight best-seller. I had spent the last months defending the characteristic of God's justice because I believed it was consistent with what the Bible teaches about God and is consistent with the historic teaching of the global church. Furthermore, I know how much we need a God who is just and governs justly. I spent much time helping people work through how the Bible teaches us that those guilty of rape, corruption, genocide, murder and abuse would all be held accountable by God one day. The Christian worldview has much to draw from assuring us that a world crying out for justice will be answered and satisfied.

This chapter is not written in order for us to decide whether or not we *like* the doctrine of Hell, but rather to explore whether or not it is consistent with a God who could be both perfectly loving and still allow people to spend eternity separated from him. We will also look at the rationale for the existence of Hell. I will argue that it is very reasonable for God to ordain a place where those who freely reject him will go and not be with him.

I will also argue that we need the promise of a just God enforcing justice in our world. We can be thankful for the many Bible promises from God that, "he will not let the guilty go unpunished" (Ex. 34:7. Num. 14:18, Is. 10:5). It can be easy from the comfort of a quiet suburb to talk about a God who would never judge anyone for anything they do. However, to a Rwanadan child who has watched his father and mother killed in cold blood with a machete, the only thing that could stop him from killing in revenge would be a high view of God's justice. His rage and drive for vengeance would naturally lead him to take an "eye for an eye." Alternatively, he could end the cycle of violence with a settled confidence in the one who tells us, "Vengeance is mine" (Rom. 12:19).

The Bible promises us that we don't have to settle our own scores; "God is just: He will pay back trouble to those who trouble you" (2 Thess. 1:6). Instead, we can trust a just God to do this and try our best to leave at peace with people.

WE NEED A GOD WHO JUDGES

Some people may still not be convinced about the existence of Hell. What if they are right? What if there is no right and wrong, and it follows, nobody to enforce justice. You would not want that. Consider this example. Picture for yourself the most violent, disgustingly perverted, tyrannical ruler from any time in history. He abuses his slaves with inhumane working conditions, forces them to work long hours and offers no days off. He tortures anyone who goes against him, and for his whole career, has made extra money embezzling funds from his people. As a result, these people live and die in poverty and squalor.

Now picture that after decades of this sort of oppression, brutality, and abuse, that this guy is dying in a bed right in front of you. Desperate for breath, yet still hanging on to the little life he has, he motions for you to come close. The dying old crook wants to tell you something. He recalls with a sly snicker all the women he slept with and quickly cast aside afterwards. He tells you how rich he got at the expense of the workers and the poor. He tells you with pride how he tortured his enemies, often killing them in front of their children to show his power and ensure their future submission. Going on like this, his tone is boastful, proud and defiant of any power in heaven or on earth. With his last bit of energy he laughs,

"And I got away with all of it."

To whom or to what does your sense of justice appeal at this moment? You want this man to be held accountable for the cruel, corrupt way he lived his life. But will it happen? The Christian's view of a God who holds *everyone* accountable seems very appealing at this point. You are thankful that there is no amount of earthly power or wealth that will be able to get him out of this one.

When the Bible talks about how God will ultimately judge sin one day, I insist that this is good news. What would we do without accountability for sin? Should rapists, murderers, thieves, pedophiles, liars, cheaters, bullies, drug dealers, corrupt governments, greedy CEOs, and terrorists never have to be held accountable for their actions? Should they be able to just keep hurting people without a final judgment for the evil they have done? That is not the world in which I would want to live.

A WORD OF CAUTION

As human beings, we must take a humble position here. We must be careful not to place ourselves above God and serve as judges on his behalf. Psalm 115:3 is clear that God can do whatever he pleases. He informs us in Isaiah 55:9 that his ways are far different from ours. Not only are they different but, because he is God, his ways are superior.

It is also important to establish where this argument lies in defense of the Christian faith. It is a moral argument safely nestled *within* a universe in which God already exists. You cannot say, "I cannot believe in God because he lets people go to Hell." This is mistakenly blending two different categories of argument. It is like saying, "My boss does not exist because I do not like the way he runs the company." It does not work logically. First you have to answer the question, "Does God exist?" and then (given the existence of God) work through what he is like.

Concerning the Christian doctrine of Hell, we will see that, when taught correctly, it does not point to a brutish tyrannical deity. Instead, it reveals a holy, loving and gracious God who, *thankfully,* has standards which allow freedom of choice and justice for all.

Let's take a look at what God is like as he describes himself in the pages of the Bible.

GOD'S HOLINESS

All revelation must start with God. In the Bible, God has revealed to us what he is like. One of the attributes of God that the Bible most often celebrates is his holiness. God has called himself the "Holy One of Israel" (Ps. 71:22, 78:41, 89:18, Isa.1:4 , 5:19, 24 et al.). In God's presence are countless heavenly creatures declaring that he is "holy, holy, holy". This attribute, they feel, is most worthy of worship (Isa. 6:3). The Psalmist cries out, "The LORD our God is holy!" (Ps. 99:9). Wayne Grudem helps us understand what this characteristic of God is telling us:

> God's holiness means that he is separated from sin and devoted to seeking his own honor. This definition contains both a relational quality (separation from) and a moral quality (the separation is from sin or evil, and the devotion is to the good of God's own honor or glory).[104]

According to the above definition, the second aspect of God's holiness reflects his morality. If you are holy, then all you do is holy. This is good news for us because we know that God will always do the right thing. His nature is trustworthy. His decisions are consistently right and good. Honestly, I cannot say the same about the decisions we humans make.

OUR CHOICE

How we respond to God's invitation of relationship is our choice. God made us with the ability to accept him or reject him.

---

[104] Wayne Grudem. *Systematic Theology* (Grand Rapids, Mich.: Zondervan, 2010).

He respects the choices of his own creation so much that he is willing to let people run away from him. Deeply embedded in the Christian worldview is the truth that God gave us an invitation to choose him or reject him. We have chosen (and still choose) to reject him. The early pages of Genesis record that our first parents, Adam and Eve, were the first ones to disobey the command of God. At the root it was not about eating bad fruit. It was all about rebellion. They chose to be their own gods rather than obeying the true God (see Genesis 3:5). Their choice to reject that which is holy instantly made them unholy. For this choice they were cast out of the garden paradise, Eden. Banishment from Eden is a picture of the spiritual reality that would affect all humanity from that point onward. Romans 5:12 teaches us that "just as sin came into the world through one man, and death through sin, and so death spread to all men because all sinned."

All sinned? If this is true, then it does make sense of many things. It explains why you do not have to teach kids to be selfish. It explains why you do not have to teach nations to go to war with each other. It also explains why the city of Vancouver hired riot police before Stanley Cup finals and not "spontaneous acts of kindness, compassion and love" police. The city anticipated outbursts of chaos and violence from many humans getting together.[105]

More personally, sin explains my own rebellious heart towards God. It explains why I default toward being selfish, mean, proud and hard-hearted to the things of God and towards others.

Every worldview has to reconcile the fact that something has gone wrong with the world. Christians believe that everyone has been deeply affected by sin. Sin is a violation of the good order that God has hard-wired into his universe. Because we have all sinned, it is the great equalizer of humanity's condition before God. The most down to earth people I know are most aware of

---

[105] Steve Kroeker. *The Hero*, (Tsawassen, BC.) 2011.

their own failure to be good. Peter Kreeft observes, "Sinners think they are saints, but saints know they are sinners."[106]

You must understand that I am not comparing the goodness of one person to the bad behaviour of another. I am not comparing people to other people at all. When most people are confronted with their sin, they will quickly appeal to the fact that they are better than many people they know. Sometimes they point. This is to miss the point entirely.[107] When we want to know if we are good, we need to see that the standard of goodness is not other people but God. Who could compete with that?

When I speak at summer camps, I enjoy playing sports with the campers. I do this to bond with them and to boost my confidence that I can demolish a ten year old in any sport. Playing soccer against junior campers (9-12 year olds), I truly dominate the soccer pitch. Against them, my head is high because I feel my soccer abilities are strong. If you put me against a striker from the English Premier League, I am much less impressive and far more humble. It's really all about with whom you are comparing yourself. Jesus says that only God is good (Mark 10:18). This means that your appeal to being a part of true, genuine goodness involves becoming a part of the Trinity. I wish you the best getting into that exclusive club.[108]

Christians are prohibited from splitting the world into good people and bad people. The Bible assures us that none of us is good, and all of us are bad. Based on what we do with Jesus, our response divides us into two groups; not good people and bad people: but forgiven people and unforgiven people. There are those who receive the offer of mercy and grace for sin and those

---

[106] Peter Kreeft. "The Problem Of Evil" www.peterkreeft.com/topics/evil.htm Accessed September 17, 2012.

[107] Pun intended.

[108] Thanks to *Ravi Zacharias International Ministries* speaker, Michael Ramsden, for help with that joke.

who continue to resist their need or desire for it. Their stubbornness and refusal to submit to Jesus echoes the blasphemous tone of the poet, William Ernest Henle. In his poem, *Invictus* he writes:

> It matters not how strait the gate,
> How charged with punishments the scroll.
> I am the master of my fate:
> I am the captain of my soul.

The Bible is clear that heaven is all about the celebration of the centrality and victory of Jesus. If you spent your life declaring autonomy from God, would you want to spend eternity with him when you die? We know that Joseph Stalin fiercely rejected God and the people of God for his entire life. At his death bed, those nearby said that Stalin shook his fist to the heavens moments before breathing his last. Would Stalin be the kind of guy who would enjoy heaven? I believe God lets people like Stalin, those who want nothing to do with him, have their way. C.S. Lewis writes in his book, *The Great Divorce*, "There are those who say to God, 'Thy will be done' and those to whom God says, 'Thy will be done.'"[109] These are the ones who are deceived like the fallen angels in Milton's famous work, *Paradise Lost*. They are convinced that it is better to reign in Hell, than serve Jesus in Heaven.[110]

When I discuss Hell with people it seems to me that, with them, God can never win. For example, God could take away our free will so that every human decision could never be wrong nor could anyone do any wrong. He could program us to always make the right decision at the right time. If he did this, we would conclude that he is a cosmic micro-manager. We would condemn him for making a world in which every decision we make is predetermined and therefore, pointless. On the other hand, God

---

[109] C.S. Lewis. *The Great Divorce*. (Harper Collins, New York, NY, 1946).

[110] John Milton. *Paradise Lost*. Public Domain. Line 263.

could allow people to have real choices with real consequences depending on what we choose to do. This would include the ability for people to choose acts of love and bravery but also acts of evil.

If God allowed this chosen evil to carry on without any consequences, we would criticize him for being weak and governing an unjust world. That's what we do all the time with our own government's criminal justice system.

Furthermore, because God is just when he judges evil and punishes the evildoer, we condemn him for being harsh and cruel. We either criticize him for not letting us make decisions, or we criticize him for allowing them.

This shows that no matter what God does, people seem to naturally take issue and shake their fists at him. It tells less about God and more about the hard-hearted stubbornness of rebellious human beings. It also serves as more evidence for the effects of a fallen humanity: we desire to be our own gods, thinking that we know better than God. This is human folly at its utmost.

THE FOLLY OF MAN'S REBELLION

Sin destroys us in the same way that orange juice in a gas tank will destroy a car. Your car was designed to run on gasoline; anything else other than its original design will break it down. Since we were not made to sin, it breaks down our lives as well. In fact, any attempt to go against God's natural laws will result in severe damage. Allow me to illustrate with this cartoon.[111]

---

[111] Thanks to *Ravi Zacharias International Ministries* President, Michael Ramsden, for an illustration idea that inspired this cartoon

GUILTY UNTIL PROVEN BROKEN

Peter did not like physics class. It's not that he was one of those kids who didn't like school; he just didn't agree with what was being taught.

The teacher taught such a narrow-minded perspective on topics such as gravity. Peter did not like his teacher's arrogance when he insisted that everything that goes up must come down.

Wanting to disprove his teacher (and the law of gravity), Peter put on a cape and climbed to the top of his house. He jumped off and went straight into the ground, head first. Thankfully, he had also worn a helmet that day.

Peter never broke the laws of gravity that day. He only broke his helmet. If this was not a made up story, he would also have broken his neck. He was back in school for the next physics lesson.

FRICTION

Still not totally sold on physics, Peter attended the next class determined to put the laws of friction to the test. He did not like the idea that gravity and mass could reduce kinetic energy causing moving objects to slow down and stop.

Peter went to his local ice rink, strapped butter to his feet and slid across the ice. When he crashed into the boards, his kinetic energy was absorbed and gravity slowly pulled him to the ice. He never broke the laws of friction - just his nose, a leg and and an arm.

The doctor told Peter to rest. Peter did not like the idea of rest. He did not like the doctor's rigid rules. He thought he could disprove the laws of rest.

Peter stayed up all night. Eventually he got so tired that he passed out in class.
If time permitted it, we could talk about all the other laws that Peter wanted to disprove. Instead of breaking them, he ended up being a very broken young man.

Thankfully, this story has a happy ending. Finally, more aware of the truth and relevance of the laws of nature, Peter understood physics better than any others in his class. His body eventually healed, and he became an excellent physics teacher.

THE END

Peter learned that there are certain laws woven into the fabric of the way this world works. When he tried to break them, he only ended up proving them and being broken down himself. That's how sin works. Sin is a violation of God's created order. Sin is taking the way God has set up the world and perverting, distorting or disobeying it. You have to see sin as a self-selected rebellion against the created order of the universe. We insist, like Peter, on trying to break that order. Instead, it breaks us in the process.

Hell is a necessary component of the eventual consequences for our own foolish choices to rebel against God and the way he has designed the world to run. Thankfully, God has given us time to turn from our foolish rebellion against him and to seek to obey him instead.

WHY GOD WAITS

A friend of mine recalled an event from the Canada versus USA gold medal hockey game in the 2010 Winter Olympics. In the first period, American player Bobby Ryan clearly tripped up a Canadian player while he was chasing after the puck. This kind of thing is against the rules of hockey. All the fans in the arena and all over the nation of Canada screamed out for justice in this moment. Immediately all eyes went to the referee to see if he would call it. Was he the sort of referee who would allow the rules of hockey to be broken? Did he care if rules were broken? Would he let the Americans get away with it?

The referee put his hand up as the game continued. Though no call was made, all of Canada exhaled their tension knowing that they would get justice for the unjust infraction against their player, their team and their nation (true Canadians know I'm not being dramatic here). In hockey, a referee with his/her hand up is a signal to show a penalty is coming... eventually. Once the penalized team touches the puck, the referee blows the whistle, and the penalty is called. The Americans eventually got their penalty. Canada would go on to win the game, the gold medal and thus retain international hockey supremacy for the next four years.

God is clear that he, the judge, has his hand up against all those who do evil in this world. Like the good referee from the gold medal game, he sees all infractions and will call the penalty once the whistle goes. Until then, he waits. He waits so that he will be able to show grace and mercy to the maximum number of people. While people are still alive, they still have time to repent of their sin and turn to Jesus for grace.

But be assured — he will not wait forever.

WHAT ABOUT AFTER-DEATH SECOND CHANCES?

There are some theologians, pastors and authors who are tragically mistaken and put forward the idea that if people deny Jesus in this life, God will give them another chance to repent of their sin once they die. They argue that in the end, everyone will eventually come to repentance and that Hell will be emptied one day. I believe that the proponents of this view may have their hearts in the right place, but I am saddened that their brains are not so fortunate. I admit that I want them to be right. I really do. I do not want Hell for anyone. However, no passage in the Bible teaches that there will be a second chance for people after they die.[112] Since passages in the New Testament like Luke 13:22-30, Hebrews 9:27 and others seem to teach the exact opposite to this kind of post-mortem repentance, it is especially frightening that some Christians would hold this view. How tragic it would be to go about one's life holding to this view and then to stand before God only to find out you were wrong. My advice to those who are concerned with the idea of people going to Hell is rather than trying to deny it, do *everything you can* on this side of eternity to stop anyone from experiencing it. You can do this by

---

[112] For more on this check out Francis Chan's book *Erasing Hell: What God Has Said About Eternity And The Things We Made Up* (Colorado Springs, CO : David Cook, 2011).

telling them about the love and grace of Jesus and modeling his unending love for them.

Let's summarize what we have learned thus far. God is the supreme Ruler of this world. He is holy, and nothing can ever compromise this important aspect of his nature. Human beings, because of their choices to sin against God, become unholy. This is a problem for us because God is also just. God will rightfully judge anything that would seek to go against his rule, his laws, or his holiness. This kind of governance, as we have learned, is something that humans appreciate in our authorities. In the case of the evil we observed in the world, I have argued, we need to appreciate God's justice as well.

It seems that rather than ask how a good God could possibly allow anyone to go to Hell, the better question seems to be,

How could a holy and just God allow anyone to go to heaven?

The only way to answer this is that God is not only holy and just but, thankfully, he is also loving.

WHEN GOD JUDGES HIMSELF

The way that God saves us from getting the punishment for our sins is through punishing himself. We get mercy not by God's excluding his need for justice but *through* his justice. In the first century AD, Jesus died on a Roman cross just outside of Jerusalem. It was there that Jesus absorbed the wrath of God for our sin. Jesus paid the debt of sin that no good work of our own could pay. On the cross, the attributes of God were on display for all to see. The justice of a holy God was satisfied as a payment for sin through the death of his Son. The love, mercy and grace of God were also displayed there as Jesus willingly laid down his life for all who would receive him. "For God so loved the world he gave his only son that *whoever believes in him should not perish but have eternal life*" (John 3:16, my emphasis).

The unfathomable miracle is that God has provided us a way back to him. The sad thing is that people get upset that he has not provided more ways. It seems to me that if God offered ten ways back to him, people would complain that he did not offer eleven.

Here is the truth about sin: either Jesus pays for your sin or you pay for it yourself. When people resist God's offer of grace, he has reserved a place for them. It is a place where they will not have to worry about his trying to interfere with their business any longer. I see that Hell is reasonably ordained by a God who honours a person's choice to reject him.

CONCLUSION

It is much easier to write books saying that Hell is not something people need to worry about anymore. The problem is that such books will be of little help to you when you stand before God one day. In this chapter I have shown why the Christian doctrine of Hell is necessary as a consequence of a human being's free will rejection of God. Hell is also an eternal punishment for sin in accordance with an eternal and just God who governs the universe justly. Hell is talked about in the Bible and throughout the history of orthodox Christianity.

When discussing this topic, it can be easy to get thinking about all the other kinds of people who really deserve it. We have talked in this chapter about evil tyrants, corrupt national leaders, thieves, rapists and murderers. Thankfully, the doctrine of Hell speaks of consequences for such injustices. It also speaks to us "ordinary sinners" as well. God judges sin.

Do you ever sin? Justice gets very personal all of a sudden. There are passages in the Bible that are clear about the judgment we will all face after this life. Hebrews 9:27 informs us, "...it is appointed for man to die once, and after that comes judgment." Either these kinds of verses are true or they are not. If these words are true, we best get right with God on his terms. He has provided salvation through his Son Jesus Christ and through none other.

As one who cares about you, I have taken the time to write this out for you. I have chosen to tell you why Hell is a controversial and yet key part of the Christian worldview. It is your job to make a decision about what you will do about it. The same choice humanity was given in the garden of Eden is now the choice that you have to make - will you accept God's invitation of relationship or will you reject it?

I conclude this chapter with the fitting insight of C.S. Lewis regarding the rationality of the Christian doctrine of Hell:

> In the long run the answer to all those who object to the doctrine of Hell is itself a question: 'What are you asking God to do?' To wipe out past sins and, at all costs, to give them a fresh start, smoothing every difficulty and offering every miraculous help? But he has done so, on Calvary. To forgive them? They will not be forgiven. To leave them alone? Alas, I am afraid that is what He does.[113]

---

[113] C.S. Lewis. *The Problem Of Pain*. (Harper Collins, New York, NY, 1940).

THE RESURRECTION OF JESUS:
THE DAY THAT CHANGED EVERYTHING

"If Christ has not been raised, your faith is futile; you are still in your sins. Then those who have fallen asleep in Christ are lost. If only for this life we have hope in Christ, we are to be pitied more then all men."
-1 Corinthians 15:12–20

I have been asked before if there is anything that could be discovered that would destroy my faith as a Christian. There is something that would accomplish that. If they found Jesus' body, thus proving that he remained dead in the grave, I would have to give up my faith. Paul Johnson agrees, "Christianity is essentially an historical religion. It bases its claims on the historical facts it asserts. If these are demolished, it is nothing."[114]

---

[114] Paul Johnson. *A History of Christianity*, (New York: Touchstone, 1976), vii

Skeptic Carl Sagan thought he was condemning Christianity when he said that, "Extraordinary claims demand extraordinary evidence." Though my skeptic friends try to use this comment against Christianity, I think Sagan's statement is in full agreement with what the Bible is telling us. Extraordinary claims *do* demand extraordinary evidence! The Bible openly admits that if Jesus is dead, Christianity is also dead with him (1 Cor. 15:14). Anybody can claim to be God. The real question comes in whether or not they can back their claim up. To do so effectively, they would need to pull off something big. Christians claim that Jesus backed up his extraordinary claim with an extraordinary resurrection.

If Christians are right, that is, if Jesus is alive, it would be a historical game changer. I want to show you now why there is compelling evidence that Christianity is true because Jesus rose from the dead. With such a claim, you can tell how much is at stake in the pages of this chapter. The skeptic himself would have to admit that, if Jesus is alive, then that also affirms some other truths about Christianity such as:

- There is a God, and he can do miracles like raising someone from the dead.
- Jesus affirmed the authority of the Bible. If Jesus is alive, he is God, and what he said about the Bible is true.
- If Jesus is alive, we can better understand the problem of evil. Though we may not always understand why evil is so prevalent, if Jesus is alive, we can be confident that he has dealt with it.

These big apologetic questions all bottleneck into this one question:

Did Jesus of Nazareth really rise from the dead?

There are good reasons to be skeptical about this claim. Resurrections are not a part of our normal experience. In fact, if someone wanted to research resurrections, they could go to a graveyard every day for a whole year and carefully observe if any resurrections were happening. After a full year of collected data I am confident the resurrection count would read "Zero." My suspicions are that the researcher would then conclude that resurrections are im...*probable*.

The overwhelming majority of people who die do not rise from the dead. That is as far as the research can take someone on that point. History contains an account of one resurrection after death that must be taken into consideration as part of this study.

For those who struggle with doubts about God, one of the most encouraging stories in the gospels is the story of the disciple, Thomas. In John's gospel, Thomas is famously skeptical about the report that Jesus was alive again. Resurrections, in his mind, were on the list of *Things That Do Not Happen*. He announces to the group of witnesses, "Unless I see in his hands the mark of the nails, and place my finger into the mark of the nails, and place my hand into his side, I will never believe" (John 20:25). Thomas would only believe that which could be physically proven.

I appreciate that Jesus cared enough about Thomas' questions to visit him personally. This encounter tells us much about how Jesus is so gracious to us when we are going through our own doubt. Jesus confronted Thomas with the evidence, and Thomas had to choose what to do with the information. Thomas makes his choice. In the presence of the resurrected Jesus, he erupts in worship, "My Lord and my God!" (John 20:28). Perhaps Jesus knew that many would come later who would be in a similar situation as Thomas, full of doubt but without having Jesus physically standing there to touch. Jesus wants to bless them, "Have you [Thomas] believed because you have seen me? Blessed are those who have not seen and yet have believed."

Jesus said that those who do not get the once-in-history opportunity to put their hands in his wounds would still be blessed. From now on, they would have the historic evidence as this chapter will explain. As a bonus, they would have the presence of the Holy Spirit leading them into truth. I would encourage you not to neglect either as you explore where you land on this claim.

Is something like a resurrection possible? The question first takes us to the nature of miracles. Does the world we live in function within a closed system where no miracles can happen, or do we live in an open universe into which God is able to intervene?

A WORD ABOUT MIRACLES

To many people, miracles are completely off the table. For them the universe functions as a closed system. Naturalism is the belief that nature is the ultimate reality, and nothing can interrupt or disrupt the way it runs. There is no room for talk of the *super*natural. It is outside of the naturalist's *modus operandi*. This worldview argues that since there are natural laws that govern the way things happen every time. In fact, those laws govern the way things happen *every time with out any outside help*.

If there is a God, as theists believe, he can certainly be involved in his created world. The question quickly shifts to the existence of such a being. "Is there a God who can do miracles or not?" This is why this book started with the numerous evidences that point to the existence of God. I believe theism is the most rational explanation for the world we experience. If there is a God, he can do whatever he wants, whenever he wants in history. Richard Swinburne explains, "natural laws can be set aside only by the action or with the permission of God who sustains them in operation."[115]

It is a given that miracles are an anomaly. They are not what we usually experience. They are God's to give and not ours to demand from him. However, God often chooses to intervene like

---

[115] Richard Swinburne. *The Existence Of God* (Oxford, Eng. Oxford University Press). p282

this. In this chapter we are really looking at only one historical miracle: The miracle of God raising Jesus from the dead, three days after he was crucified. The following paragraphs are what have led me and many others to believe this is what happened.

THE CIRCUMSTANTIAL EVIDENCE

In a court case, a jury is assigned the very serious role of considering all the evidence that was collected and presented by both the plaintiff and the defendant. The jury then makes a decision based on what they believe "beyond reasonable doubt" to be true. The case that is made, a collection of all that points to the guilty (or not guilty) party, is called "circumstantial evidence." This is what we will look at regarding the resurrection of Jesus. What is the evidence that supports Jesus being alive?

The resurrection of Jesus is the lynchpin of the Christian faith. In light of the evidence, Sir Lionel Luckhoo, the man deemed by the *Guinness Book Of World Records* as "the most successful lawyer in history" has this to say about it:

> I say unequivocally that the evidence for the resurrection of Jesus Christ is so overwhelming that it compels acceptance by proof which leaves absolutely no room for doubt.[116]

In 1 Corinthians 15:1-9, we get a sense that Paul shares a similar conviction. Here he builds a case for the resurrection for his original audience, the church that met in the city of Corinth. Paul appeals to authorities, testimonies, eyewitnesses, and his own experience as evidence for the Corinthians to consider. He says to them, "What I received, I pass on to you." I would express similar sentiments. What I have received from the likes of

---

[116] As quoted in *Who Made God?* Edited by Norman Geisler and Ravi Zacharias. (Grand Rapids, Mich : Zondervan Publishing, 2003). p. 97

scholars like Gary Habermas, Mike Licona, William Lane Craig and my friend, Chris Price, I now pass on to you.

The Changed Life of Peter

Peter was one of Jesus' closest friends. He was "one of the three" with whom Jesus spent most of his time. In the gospel accounts, Peter clearly shows leadership amongst the other disciples. Jesus knows Peter is secure enough to make an example of him at times. Having spent so much time with Jesus, Peter had a front row seat on occasions when Jesus foretold his death and resurrection. Since Peter was there to hear all this, he should have been the one disciple who, after Jesus' burial, was the most expectant of his return (just as Jesus promised him). Peter should have been parked in front of Jesus' tomb sitting on a lawn chair with a bucket of popcorn reassuring everyone, "Don't worry everyone, he told me he'll be back soon."

The Bible tells us that this was not Peter's experience. What happened instead is that after the arrest of Jesus, this disciple did not want to be associated with his friend. Denying him three times, once even to a little peasant girl, Peter's cowardice was on full display. If you are a gospel writer trying to make up an impressive story, it is unlikely that you would include this embarrassing episode in Peter's life, unless, of course it was exactly how it all happened.

Following the resurrection, a new man emerges. No longer the cowardly denier of Jesus, Peter is now the bold street preacher exposing the sin of the Jewish people and the triumph of King Jesus. Peter would suffer greatly for this transformation. The accounts of early church fathers Origen, Tertullian and St. Clement inform us that Peter's allegiance to Jesus would cost him his life. Like his friend Jesus, Peter would die by crucifixion.

What kind of event would explain such a change in Peter? Something as drastic as a friend rising from the dead would be a sufficient explanation. In 1 Corinthians 15, Paul suggests that

Peter's story is good evidence that Jesus is alive. It was not just Peter's life that we are told to consider. Consider all the other lives that met the resurrected Jesus as well.

The Changed Lives of the Disciples

If you went through airport security in August of 2001, took a flight to an uninhabited island for a month and came through another airport in October, you would observe that something dramatic had happened while you were gone. Something caused a major policy shift. In August of 2001, I remember walking calmly through lazily guarded airport security X-ray machines en route to board a plane. In October of that same year, it was a much different story. Instead of breezing by, I was being stripped, groped and robbed of my precious 150ml tubes of toothpaste. Security at all international airports was beefed up like never before. Billions of dollars were poured into upgrading these checkpoints. Restrictions on what could and could not be taken on an airplane were strictly enforced. These rules caused long lineups which frustrated travelers. What could catalyze such a change in security protocol? The explanation that people gave then, and will give forever, was that on September 11, 2001, two airplanes were highjacked and flown into the World Trade Center buildings in Manhattan, New York.

September 11 forever changed airports.

The resurrection of Jesus forever changed the eyewitnesses.

For many generations before Jesus came, the Jewish people longed for freedom over the occupying Roman forces that were oppressing the nation of Israel. They awaited the promised Messiah who was supposed to overthrow the Romans and reestablish Israel as a powerful nation. For a long time, it would have looked like Jesus was the guy to do it. Confirmed by his miracles, he healed people, fed multitudes, calmed storms, and walked on water. He even turned water to wine. One can easily see why Jesus could always draw a crowd. Jesus lived and

161

talked like he was Israel's promised Messiah. Hope was climaxing but was suddenly squelched when Jesus was crucified by the very Romans he was supposed to overthrow. No angels came to his rescue. He pulled off no eleventh hour heroics. He just hung there and died.

We do not know much about what the disciples did in the following days. We are told that they scattered when Jesus was arrested, and few showed up for his crucifixion. From his view on the cross, the last Jesus saw of his disciples was the backs of their heads as they ran away. We see a glimpse of the despair they must have all felt in the conversation of two dejected disciples as they walked along a road to a town called Emmaus. "We thought he was the one to redeem Israel" (Luke 24:21).

Again, if you are making up this story, you do not include the bits where the main characters show such weakness. After all, these dejected men are none other than soon-to-be-members of the early church's core leadership team.

Some days later, the gospels tell us that these same disciples were worshipping Jesus as God. Strict monotheistic Jews would have had to quickly readjust their theological paradigms after the resurrection. It is clear that they knew that there was a God and that Jesus was that God! Not only did they believe it themselves, they went about boldly proclaiming the Messiah had come and that the Messiah was Jesus, the man from Nazareth. They, too, like Peter, were persecuted for this claim. They were kicked out of synagogues and most of them were killed for their belief in the resurrection.

Do not blink, or you will miss the change in these disciples. How did this group of cowards transform into courageous martyrs? They changed their behaviour because they had encountered the resurrected Jesus. The truth that would forever change the trajectory of human history was standing there, talking to them, cooking with them, eating with them. Jesus was back! No longer could they doubt him; no longer would they be ashamed of him.

The changed lives of the disciples is good evidence to believe in the resurrection of Jesus. If that group of twelve does not convince you, how about another five hundred?

The Five Hundred Eyewitnesses

The eyewitnesses to the atrocities that happened in Nazi death camps are the most authoritative voices against anyone who would deny that the Holocaust happened. Today, those who have survived the Holocaust are long into old age, and few are still alive. If anyone wanted to know what it was like in Nazi concentration camps, the best person to talk to would be those who experienced it firsthand. Paul understood the power of eyewitness testimony. He uses it in his defence of the resurrection. After name dropping Peter and the disciples, Paul plays the numbers card to strengthen his argument: "Then he [the resurrected Jesus] appeared to more than five hundred" (1 Cor. 15:6).

Paul refers to this large, aging group and says to the Corinthians, "Many of these people are still alive - you can go and talk to them yourself! I can give you names and addresses!" In his book, *Jesus and The Eye Witnesses*, Richard Baukham has done excellent work showing how important eyewitness accounts were in first century literature. Eyewitness testimony was considered the most important source and carried the most weight.[117]

As secular and liberal historians scramble to discredit Baukham's work, I believe as many do today, that the testimony of eye-witnesses is the best way to credit or discredit a claim. Whether it be a witness to a crime, the testimony of a Holocaust survivor, or the witness of a resurrection, simply adding time (in this case two thousand years) to their testimony does not change

---

[117] Richard Baukham. *Jesus And The Eyewitnesses* (Grand Rapids, Mich.: Eerdmans Publishing, 2006). p26.

the trustworthiness of the information. Eyewitness testimony was a priority then, and it remains as such to us today.

When you Believe your Brother is God

I am an older brother, and I know that it would take an awful lot to convince my younger brother that I am God and worthy of his worship. Granted, his childhood would have been much more satisfying for him if he had conceded to a routine of elder brother worship. At the time of writing, he has yet to bow the knee. The Bible tells us that Jesus also had brothers who were just as reluctant to worship him (Mark 6:3, Matt. 13:55). His mother Mary may have been a virgin when she had Jesus, but it is clear that she did not stay that way.[118] For Jesus' first brother, James, to worship him as God and devote himself to a life of service in the church is a very big deal. It is a much bigger deal than we probably realize. Paul gives these five quick words, but they really are a miracle when you consider how rare sibling worship is. "Then he appeared to James." (1 Cor. 15:7).

What would you do if your sibling confessed his or her divinity to you? That would surely make for some awkward Thanksgiving dinners. In Mark 3:31, Jesus is preaching, and his family is said to be waiting outside for him to finish. At various other points in the early stages of Jesus' ministry, his brothers seem quite skeptical and apathetic about their brother's divine claim (Mt. 13:57; Mk. 3:21, 6:4; Jn. 7:5). Since Jesus represented the whole family in a Middle Eastern shame culture, they were, no doubt, embarrassed by the kind of mixed attention their controversial brother was getting.

---

[118] For more on this see J.P. Meier, *A Marginal Jew: Rethinking the Historical Jesus*, Vol. 1 (New York: Doubleday, 1991), pp. 316-332; For a critique of Meier's arguments, see R. Bauckham, 'The Brothers and Sisters of Jesus: An Epiphanian Response to John P. Meier', *Catholic Biblical Quarterly* 56 (1994), 686-700.

However, all that changed at some point. James became one of the leaders in the Jerusalem church, the hub of the emerging Christian movement. He had a position of unrivalled authority in those early days of the church. Josephus records that James' leadership led to his martyrdom by stoning under the high priest Ananus II in 62AD.[119]

What brought about such a change in James? What caused him to go from a skeptical brother to a willing martyr? I agree with Paul that the most probable explanation is that the resurrected Jesus appeared to his brother.

Paul's Personal Testimony

Jesus taught us to love our neighbours even when they do not love us. Richard Dawkins lived about a block away from my old room at Wycliffe Hall in Oxford. When Dawkins was out walking his dog, I always made a point of saying hello. He was always cordial to me, but I know how he talks about people like myself. He does not like Christians. He thinks we are plagued with a "religious virus" and has made it part of his life's mission to eradicate this virus from the earth. I would love Dawkins to see Jesus, not as his favourite problem with the world, but acknowledge as the Creator, Saviour and King. I imagine that if Richard Dawkins did convert to Christianity, this would be very shocking news to all.

When the Apostle Paul gave his life to Jesus, I think people would have had a similar reaction. Scripture records, "And all who heard him were amazed and said, 'Is not this the man who made havoc in Jerusalem of those who called upon this name?'" (Acts 9:21).

Paul was a fierce persecutor of Christians. He hated them and wanted to have them killed. Paul tells the Galatians, "For you have heard of my former life in Judaism, how I persecuted the

---

[119] Josephus, *Antiquities* 20.200.

church of God violently and tried to destroy it" (Gal. 1:13). Acts 9 records Paul's dramatic and sudden conversion to Christianity, a conversion which he later understated to the Corinthians. "He [the resurrected Jesus] appeared also to me" (15:9) was all he says of the conversion story that would forever change history. Paul went from a man on a mission to destroy churches to a fearless man on a mission to plant them! This would cost the converted apostle everything, including his very life. For Paul, the appearance of the resurrected Jesus was enough to compel such a change at such a cost.

Jesus' appearance to Peter, the disciples, the five hundred eyewitnesses, James and Paul all serve as evidence in Paul's resurrection apologetic to the Corinthian church. There is still more evidence for us to consider before we must declare our own verdict.

Day of the Week for Worship Changed

Allow me to speak a little tongue-in-cheek for a moment. I grew up in church, have worked many years in a church, and will spend the rest of my life serving the church. When I am critical of church people, realize that I am criticizing my own family here. I have many criticisms of this group. My two for now are as follows: Our coffee is consistently second-rate and church people despise change. This is why, no matter how much I complain about the coffee, it never changes. The only place you're going to find changes in church are in the nursery. Church babies are the only ones who like changes!

There was one historic change that was so drastic that something drastic must have happened to catalyze it. During the time of his ministry, we see that Jesus and his disciples were comfortable meeting in Jewish synagogues on the Sabbath day (Saturday). Once Jesus was resurrected, Christians started meeting on Sundays instead. They called it, "The Lord's Day." We read this in early literature as such letters from Pliny the Elder, the *Didache* or the historical writings of Eusebius. Justin Martyr, writing in the second century explains the Christian day of worship:

> But Sunday is the day on which we all hold our common assembly, because it is the first day on which God, having wrought a change in the darkness and matter, made the world; and Jesus Christ our Saviour on the same day rose from the dead.[120]

Though Christians may not be so keen to embrace change, an incident as dramatic as a resurrection might just push them over the edge. If you do not think this argument is compelling, attend any church's annual general meeting - you just might agree with me. Or you might be put to sleep. Or maybe both. Just bring your own coffee.

The Testimony of the Women

On resurrection Sunday, the gospels tell us that Jesus' female disciples were the first to arrive at Jesus' tomb. These women were the first to break the story to the eleven disciples. This is another part of the resurrection story that first century writers would not have included if they were making it up. In those days, a woman's testimony held no authority. It would not have been considered evidence in a court case. If you are inventing a story that you want to sell to the world (as skeptics accuse the disciples of doing), you do not begin by establishing it with the testimony of a doubting woman, or any woman for that matter. God, however, knew better. Once again, God shows that he values women so much that they were to be the first eye-witnesses of history's most dynamic miracle! These first reports spread to the disciples, rippling throughout Jerusalem which was right in the heart of all the action. This is another convincing piece of evidence at which we must look.

---

[120] Justin Martyr. *The First Apology*, chapter LXVII. Reprinted in Alexander Roberts, Ante-Nicene Christian Library (Edinburgh: T. and T. Clark, 1867) p. 66).

The Jerusalem Factor

The epicenter of the Christian movement happened in close proximity to the location of the death of Jesus. His resurrection was not reported in Galilee, Rome or Africa - but right in the heart of all the controversy. As a historian of antiquity, Paul Maier says this of the spread of the early Christian movement:

> But this [Jerusalem] is the very last place it could have started if Jesus' tomb had remained occupied, since anyone producing a dead Jesus would have driven a wooden stake through the heart of an incipient Christianity inflamed by his supposed resurrection.[121]

All it would have taken is for one of the Roman guards to walk out with Jesus' body and announce, "Ok, stop all this commotion about a dead Messiah rising; *here* is the body." That never happened. Nobody produced the body. Instead, the Christian movement started and blossomed in the heart of and throughout all Jerusalem. From there it continued to spread to the corners of the world.

Rapid Spread of Christianity

The book of Acts tells us that the resurrection was big news on the lips of the early church. What do you make of the spread of Christianity from a handful of eyewitnesses to the estimated 31.7 million throughout the Roman Empire in the next three hundred years?

Cambridge scholar, C.F. Moule, tells us there is one very compelling argument to be made by the global explosion of Christianity, "The birth and spread of Christianity remains an

---

[121] Paul Meier. "The Empty Tomb As History." *Christianity Today*. March 28, 1975. p5.

unsolved enigma for any historian who refuses to take seriously the only explanation offered by the church itself."[122] Resurrection was the early church's explanation for why people should believe in Jesus.

The church exists because the first Christians believed that Jesus rose from the dead. They were so convinced that they spread the news all over the known world. As they were spreading this news, other alternative stories were also being told by skeptics to explain what happened to Jesus' body. Those alternative stories remain with us today.

THE ALTERNATIVE EXPLANATIONS AND THEIR PROBLEMS

Skeptics have come up with other alternatives for what could have happened to the body of Jesus. Let's look at the three strongest.

1. The Body Was Stolen by the Disciples

Even the enemies of Jesus knew the tomb was empty. Historian Ron Sider concludes, "If the Christians and their Jewish opponents both agreed that the tomb was empty, we have little choice but to accept the empty tomb as an historical fact."[123] The story that the disciples stole the body from the tomb is the oldest alternative explanation to the resurrection.[124] Each for their own various reasons, contemporary critical scholars unanimously reject this hypothesis. One has to think about a motive for the disciples' stealing Jesus' body. The best way to think about motive is to make it personal. What would compel you to give up your very life? People die for causes that they believe to be

---

[122] C.F. Moule. *The Phenomenon Of The New Testament*, (London, Eng.: SCM Press, 1969) p13

[123] Ron Sider. "A Case For Easter" *HIS Magazine*, April 29, 1972, p29.

[124] See Matthew 28:13.

true, but they would not die for lies that they had invented. Philosopher Peter Kreeft asks:

> Why would the apostles lie?...If they lied, what was their motive, what did they get out of it? What they got out of it was misunderstanding, rejection, persecution, torture, and martyrdom. Hardly a list of perks.[125]

Consider the disciples' reaction after Jesus is crucified. Their preaching of the resurrection was not motivated by fame, power, or the desire to be rich. They received none of these things for their efforts. Their response was a testimony to proclaim what they had witnessed in Jerusalem, and they were willing to give their lives for it. These men were conservative, orthodox Jewish fishermen. They were the kind of guys who would give you their word, look you in the eye and seal it with a firm handshake. These are not the sort who would be prone to deceive. Based on the credibility of the martyred disciples, the conversion of genuine skeptics like Paul and James, and the changed lives of all the eyewitnesses, scholars have not taken the stolen body view seriously for two hundred years now.[126]

2. Jesus Never Really Died

A second alternative explanation is that Jesus merely fainted on the cross and then later revived himself. His later appearance to his disciples was the reason why they thought he was resurrected. This idea became popular at the beginning of the 19th century when the liberal, naturalistic era grew in influence. Beginning with Heinrich Paulus, and with forms of it revived every year at Easter on *Discovery Channel* documentaries, this hypothesis holds little power today.

---

[125] As quoted in Norman Geisler's, *I Don't Have Enough Faith To Be An Atheist*, (Wheaton, Ill, Crossway Books, 2004) pg. 275

[126] See chapter nine of Gary Habermas's, *The Historical Jesus: Evidence For The Life Of Christ.* (College Press Publishing, 1996).

The Romans were experts at execution. Roman soldiers showed up to work and killed people by crucifixion. When Roman soldiers were ordered to kill someone, they killed them. It was, after all, their job.

Perhaps Jesus only *appeared* to be dead and then recovered enough to regain consciousness after a few days. It would be quite a feat for him to move the rock that blocked his tomb and then sneak by the guards patrolling his tomb. If Jesus was to roll the stone away, the guards would have caught him and killed him; finishing him off for good. They would not have reported back to their boss that the disciples stole him (as is recorded in Matt. 28:13). It is a pretty unlikely idea that, in his weak and bloody state, Jesus limped to his disciples' house and there convinced a crowd of depressed, fearful doubters that a "resurrection miracle" had occurred. To have such an event explain the transformation of the disciples into fearless martyrs is a big ask. These points are sufficient grounds to dismiss the idea that Jesus never really died.

3. The Disciples Hallucinated

The last most prominent alternative explanation to the Christian claim that Jesus was resurrected is known as the hallucination theory.[127] This theory considers the possibility that Jesus' disciples merely thought they had seen Jesus alive when actually, he was still very dead. Though we know that individuals can be prone to hallucinations, it is highly improbable that multiple people hallucinate about the same event. The five hundred eyewitnesses that Paul references in 1 Corinthians 15:4 makes the impossibility of such a united mistake even stronger. Lastly, the hallucination theory does not

---

[127] There are other theories out there as well of which I am aware. The wrong tomb, twin and "Jesus was an alien theory" did not make the cut due to word count and a subjective plausibility limit.

take into account the claim that the tomb was empty, and Jesus' opponents have been unable to produce his body at any time.

Since history tells us that Jesus did die and was buried in a rich man's tomb and that three days later his disciples reported the tomb empty. If the disciples did not steal the body nor hallucinate into thinking they saw him, what happened to the body of Jesus? With those three eliminated as alternative explanations, one is left to either concoct other explanations or accept the conclusions for which, I believe, the evidence demands.

THE RESURRECTION IS THE BEST EXPLANATION OF THE EVIDENCE

Any alternative explanation would need to explain why Peter and the rest of the disciples transformed from cowards to radical witnesses of a bodily resurrection. It would have to explain the transformation of Paul of Damascus and why Jesus' brother worshipped him as God. Furthermore, an alternative explanation to the resurrection would have to give a reason for the credible testimony of the women disciples, the day of worship being changed to Sunday, the rapid spread of Christianity in the very center of Jerusalem, and the fact that Jesus' enemies were never able to produce his body.

If you were on a jury and this case has been made, the best explanation appears to be exactly what the Bible offers us: God raised Jesus of Nazareth from the dead. New Testament scholar Dr. N.T. Wright summarizes,

> The easiest explanation by far is that these things happened because Jesus really was raised from the dead, and the disciples really did meet him... The resurrection of Jesus does in fact provide a sufficient explanation for the empty tomb and the meetings with Jesus. Having examined all the possible hypotheses I've read about

anywhere in literature, I think it's also a necessary explanation.[128]

WHAT A RESURRECTION PROVES

Much has been said about what evidence leads us to the truth of the resurrection. The question now is, *to what does the truth of the resurrection lead us?* Let's look briefly at three of the significant implications that the empty tomb has for us today.

1. Jesus is God

One of the reasons that God would pull off such an astounding miracle as the resurrection is to put his stamp of approval on the work of his son. The Father would not have raised a heretic from the dead. As we discussed earlier, the crucifixion of Jesus, the man who claimed to be the Jewish Messiah, would have seemed like a total failure to those who witnessed it. From their perspective, no Messiah dies. Certainly no Messiah dies at the hands of his enemies. It is not always obvious to us humans which figures are worth following. Sometimes in history, God has to back up that person with a few miracles.[129] In the case of Jesus' resurrection, it was the greatest miracle. The resurrection shows Jesus' authority as a teacher, a prophet, a king, and for those who had been waiting so long for his coming, the Messiah.

2. Jesus Was Right

Jesus was often questioned about many topics. If the resurrection shows that he was God, then it also shows us that he was telling us the truth. If you witness an argument, and one person has the title of "God" as his credential, that is what we call an "authority on the subject." Jesus considered the Old Testament as words from God. They must be taken seriously. Jesus challenged the

---

[128] As quoted in, Dallas Willard's book, *Knowing Christ Today*, pg. 136

[129] Swinburne, p286.

religious leaders and told them he was bringing in a new way to relate to God, not by a change in deeds, but a change in heart. He must be right there, also. Jesus promised life to the full for all who follow him (John 10:10). He promised eternal life to all who believe in him (John 3:16). Jesus said he was the only way to God (John 14:6). It doesn't matter whether these truths suit our preferences; the resurrection tells us that he was, and still is, completely right.

3. Jesus Gives us Hope

I hate the fact that people die. It surprises me that people don't think and talk about it more because it happens to everyone at some point. Statistics show that the human mortality rate continues to hover around 100%. If you have ever experienced the death of a loved one, you know the deep grief that we feel when someone is suddenly gone. Paul wrote to the Thessalonian church about grieving in such ways, "...we do not want you to be uninformed about those who sleep in death, so that you do not grieve like the rest of mankind, who have no hope" (1 Thess. 4:13). To the Christian, there is hope in death. Death is not the end of the road. We possess a different kind of hope. What is the basis of that hope? It is the very subject of this chapter — the resurrection of Jesus. Paul continues, "For we believe that Jesus died and rose again, and so we believe that God will bring with Jesus those who have fallen asleep in him" (1 Thess. 4:14).

Theologian Nicholas Wolterstoff experienced shattering grief when his twenty-five year old son was killed in a mountain climbing accident. For Wolterstoff, the sting of death was immense. He writes of the comfort he found in his hope in the resurrection. Death, though real and painful, was never to be the end of the story. Wolterstoff's experience is well documented in his highly recommended chronicle, *Lament For A Son*. He writes:

> To believe in Christ's rising from the grave is to accept it as a sign of our own rising from our graves. If for each of us it was our destiny to be obliterated, and for all of us

together it was our destiny to fade away without a trace, then not Christ's rising but my dear son's early dying would be the logo of our fate...to believe in Christ's rising and death's dying is also to live with the power and the challenge to rise up now from all our dark graves of suffering love...So I shall struggle to live the reality of Christ's rising and death's dying. In my living, my son's dying will not be the last word.[130]

If Jesus had stayed dead, we could say that sin's ultimate consequence, death, had won. Instead, Jesus put death to death.

Unafraid of the death awaiting him, Paul taunts death in his resurrection chapter, "Where, oh Death, is your victory, where is your sting?" (1 Cor. 15:55). In the wake of the resurrection, he calls out death's power. Death offers no reply. Though we hate the reality of death, the Christian has nothing to fear either on this side of life, or on the other side of our physical death.

The resurrection is the most widely supported explanation for what happened to Jesus of Nazareth. Jesus' resurrection gives us certainty that God exists, that Jesus backed up his claims of divinity with a resurrection, and that this resurrection gives hope of eternal life to all who believe in him (John 3:16).

That is why I am a Christian.

---

[130] Nicholas Wolterstorff. *Lament for a Son*. (Grand Rapids, Mich.: Eerdman's Publishing, 1987). p92

THE PROBLEM OF EVIL:
WHOSE PROBLEM IS IT?

"Let us remember that every worldview–not just Christianity's–must give an explanation or an answer for evil and suffering...this is not just a problem distinctive to Christianity. It will not do for the challenger just to raise the question." -Ravi Zacharias

Evil is the most difficult problem in the world. It is also the strongest objection to God's existence. If God does exist, it is also the most problematic challenge to his nature and power. As a Christian, it is my greatest temptation for doubt and unbelief.

I have split my response into two sections: First, I will take the philosophical approach to this problem. We will see that there is no logical contradiction when it comes to the coexistence of God and evil. In fact, the existence of God gives necessary paradigms for calling something evil in the first place. In the following chapter I will transition to a more personal approach to the problem of evil, especially as it pertains to God's approach to our experience of suffering. If you are in the midst of a difficult period of life, you might do better skipping ahead one chapter.

RETRACING THE HORRORS OF AUSCHWITZ

I love to study history, and I am most fascinated by the great European wars of the twentieth century. The Holocaust has always been a particularly troubling time in human history for me. The word "Holocaust" comes from the Greek word "holokauston" which means "sacrifice by fire." It is the term we use to describe the killing of over six million Jews by the German Nazis during the 1930s and 40s.

Such an atrocity on earth leaves me with a question about the God of the heavens: *How could the God that I have known and loved as a truly good deity allow something as horrific as the execution of over six million Jews?* In addition to killing around 78% of the known Jewish population in occupied Germany, the Nazis executed between two and three million Russian prisoners of war, two million Poles, and many others, bringing the total up to a more likely figure of 11 million human beings.

In the spring of 2012, I got a chance to visit the death camps of Auschwitz/Burkenau. Though it was far out of the way of the path that my travel companions and I were on, I'm glad we did it. It was an experience I will never forget. Getting the chance to walk around Auschwitz made my stomach sick and my head ache.

The Holocaust Museum is located in the middle of Oświęcim, Poland, and set up so visitors can gain access into the gas chamber and crematorium where countless thousands were murdered by the Nazis. In the latter years of the war, those who entered the gates of Auschwitz were sent directly to the gas chambers. The few who were spared were forced to work in inhumane conditions. Starved and brutalized, most were dead within three months. It was surreal for me to stand in the place where tens of thousands breathed their last bit of fresh air before the last fatal one.

The Holocaust is an example of the violent capabilities of all aspects of humanity. It involved the academic world, politics, the labour force, the medical science community, the edge of technology , the passivity of the church, and the cooperation of civilians from multiple nations, races and social demographics.

My friend and I hired our own personal tour guide to take us around the museum. We heard story after story of the evil that occurred where we stood. For several hours I bombarded her with questions. I had many of them going through my head at the time (many you have probably thought as well): *How could people do this to other people? How could a God who claims to be all-powerful, all-knowing and totally good allow people to commit this kind of evil? Where is God in all this evil?*

To help answer these questions, it is best to first establish some parameters to better frame what can be called a Christian response to these questions. First we will see how, contrary to the reason given by many who leave God after experiencing something horrific, the existence of evil does not disprove God's existence. In fact, we will see how we need God to even call something "evil."

WHAT IS EVIL?

Some words we use all the time are difficult to define when we actually have to think about them. We use the word "evil" all the time but when asked to define what we are talking about, it can be quite difficult.

Think about evil as you would think of counterfeit currency. A counterfeit is the corruption of something real. You can have real currency without the existence of any counterfeits. You cannot, however, have counterfeits without the real thing existing first.

Evil is dependent on the existence of goodness but goodness is not dependent on evil.[131] Goodness was there first. It is an absolute. Evil must always be thought of in relationship with absolute goodness.

The Bible says that God is good and that he is the source of all goodness in the world. Anything that acts against God and the good he requires of us are corruptions of good. We can describe these corruptions as evil. However you define it, evil is still a problem every worldview must address at some point.

EVIL IS EVERYONE'S PROBLEM

We all understand that something is very wrong with the world. The nightly news is a perfect case study for this. Things that we think should not happen, do happen. In fact, they happen all the time. People should not hurt, kill, cheat or steal from each other. Before we go further, an embedded premise must be addressed.

The very idea (or "ideal") of what "should" happen is, in itself, a problem for a worldview that does not include God. Who is to say what should and should not happen in a world without objective, transcendent truth? If there are no moral absolutes, if there is no higher power governing the world, who has the authority to say what is right and what should happen? What standard does the atheist appeal to for how this world *should* operate?

SUFFERING AND THE PROBLEM OF ATHEISM

Atheistic evolution (by process of natural selection) depends on the suffering and extinction of weak species and the flourishing of stronger ones. It is a worldview based on the weak and poor being overcome by the strong and rich. This process, however unfortunate when played out in real life, is *necessary* for the survival of each species. The strong overcoming the weak is as

---

[131] I thank my friend, Andy Steiger, for help with this point.

natural as your need to breathe air, drink water, and eat food. On what basis then does the atheist turn on his heel and say that the world *ought not* to be full of stealing, cruelty, and doing whatever the strong need to do to overcome the weak?

Furthermore, if you are suffering *without* a belief in God, then there is not a lot of hope that your pain has any greater purpose in the grand scheme of the universe. Suffering is just a part of naturalistic evolution weeding you out of existence for something stronger and younger to take your place on the food chain.

If it is the death of someone you love, well, that happens all the time to bugs, trees, and grass. If it is sickness you are struggling with, that is survival of the fittest working out its course in you. If it is relationship sadness or loneliness, there is no one to comfort you. If you are oppressed because the government is committing genocide against your people, who will you call out to for justice? A universe without God has a response to pain; it is a helpless shoulder shrug. The big, blind, dumb, old universe simply does not care about you or your problems.

When you are suffering, that is hardly the kind of reaction you are seeking.

THE LOGICAL DEMANDS OF THE PROBLEM OF EVIL

Many Jewish people abandoned their belief in God after their experiences at Auschwitz. Suffering can do that to people. To many of my Christian friends, it did not take Auschwitz to abandon their belief in God - a divorce in the family or a bad breakup was enough for that. Adversity of all kinds makes people question God's existence. The logical truth is that there is nothing about the existence of evil that is contradictory to God's existence. For example, there is no logical problem with these two statements:

1. God Exists.

2. Evil Exists.

Granted, someone may not *like* these statements but there is no internal problem of logic here.

Then what about the problem of evil? Perhaps there is no problem at all. Perhaps we should just call it a mystery. Peter Kreeft has pointed out the difference between a problem and a mystery. A "married bachelor" is a problem. Logically, it does not work — bachelors, by definition, are *un*married. On the other hand, a bachelor who falls in love and gets married is a mystery. I have watched my best bachelor friends meet and marry wonderful girls. How these guys who fart, burp, smell, and wear shorts twelve months of the year can convince these darling ladies to marry them is a mystery to me. I can think of no other way they accomplished this than through the indescribable, mysterious human experience we call, "falling in love." When it comes to figuring out why there is so much suffering, we have to see that this is not about solving a problem of logic (How could God exist if there is evil in the world?) but a mystery to acknowledge (What reasons would God have for allowing evil in the world he made?).

Have you ever strongly believed one thing and then, with time, more information and a better perspective, found that you had to change your belief? Maybe you were repulsed by a person's decision until you asked them why they chose to do what they did. If you get an answer that seems reasonable, you might change your mind about the situation. Having more information does that to us. With God, however, he never has to change his beliefs because, at all times, he has all the information and all the perspective of eternity. I have heard countless times this critique of Christianity, "I could never believe in a God who allows such senseless evil to happen in the world." This question is loaded with understandable emotion but lacks understanding when it comes to the ability to understand what God is doing.

The skeptic has smuggled a hidden premise into this critique. That is, "If suffering *appears* senseless, then it must *be* senseless." That is an assumption beyond any human being's own capabilities. If God exists, there may be reasons he allows suffering that we, as human beings with limited knowledge, cannot discover from our perspective. The reasons are known to God but remain mysterious to us.

Imagine you get one of those dreaded phone calls that makes your guts turn. As you pick up the phone, a panicked loved one tells you that your best friend is in serious trouble. Fearing the worst, your anxiety instantly kicks in. In a twist of good fortune, you find out this friend is actually in the same building as you. If you move quickly, you might be able to save him! You take off running down a hallway, listening for clues to his location. Throwing open every door, you soon discover a light coming out from under one of the doors. Surely this is his place. Kicking open the double doors, your fears are confirmed. He is lying there with blood all over his clothes. Even worse, he is surrounded by men with knives and masks.

You yell and plead with these masked villains to stop hurting your friend. It's almost like something from a horror movie unless, of course, it isn't a horror movie at all. It is a hospital.

And the masked men with knives are doctors holding scalpels to remove the tumor that was otherwise going to kill your dear friend. Clearly, when you received the phone call you had a limited perspective. Now you know better.

In Isaiah 55:8 God tells us plainly, "'My thoughts are not your thoughts, neither are your ways my ways,' declares the Lord. 'As the heavens are higher than the earth, so are my ways higher than your ways and my thoughts than your thoughts'" (Isaiah 55:8–9).

Many times I have seen in my life, and in my friends' lives, that a seemingly terrible circumstance actually turned out to be the greatest good for those involved. Could it be possible that, from God's vantage point, there are acceptable reasons for even "bad" or "senseless" things happening?

In the Bible, the book of Job is a story that has captivated its readers for centuries. Job is a famous riches to rags kind of story. The once wealthy business and family man is reduced to ashes only to be restored to health and wealth. By the end of the book of Job, the point is clear that we simply do not know what God is up to. We do not know why he acts the way he does, but we do see that he is all good and all powerful in all he does.

The story of Joseph at the end of the book of Genesis is another story of a man who endures what seems like "meaningless suffering." As we learn in this story, Joseph's suffering turns out to be the best thing that could have happened for Joseph and many others. When Joseph was young, he told his brothers he was destined for great things. They did not respond well and threw their little brother into a well. The brothers sold young Joseph into slavery to make a few bucks off his life. Later in the story, Joseph's troubles increase. He is falsely accused of adultery with his master's wife, thrown into jail, and then forced into slave labour once again. Thankfully, like Job, things turned around for Joseph in the end. He found favour with Pharaoh and was promoted to second in command in all of Egypt. Joseph used his influence to save the nation from starvation, his family from extinction, and he was forever remembered as a part of God's redeeming plan of salvation for the world.

The great line at the end of the Joseph story is when Joseph is reunited with his brothers. Joseph has gained some impressive perspective by this point. "Do not fear", he assures them. "As for you, you meant evil against me, but God meant it for good, to bring it about that many people should be kept alive as they are today" (Gen. 50:20).

Sometimes God has his reasons for allowing suffering that we do not understand. It is not that he does not exist, it is just that we humans do not understand what he is doing. Let's look at a few reasons why God could allow evil. If there were enough plausible options, we would have to lower our raised fists and submit to God's rational but mysterious plan instead.

AN INTRODUCTION TO THE FREE WILL DEFENSE

When we ask the question of why God allows evil, we must consider that we humans are responsible for much of it. After all, human beings invented guns and bombs and are the ones who bully, cheat and hurt each other. Christian philosophers[132] have argued that a world where people can make free choices (whether for good or evil) is a better world than one in which they have no free will. The *Free-Will Defence* argues that, though people default to blaming *God* for the existence of evil, it is *humans* who commit the evil that we complain about most. What were God's options on the table regarding God's world and the human will. I have observed four:[133]

Option one is that God could have considered making a world where free people could choose evil, and they do. Once he realizes that they will choose to commit evil acts, God scraps the creation idea entirely. This is the divine fiat: "Never mind." God obviously disregarded this option, for we know that since we are here to talk about it, God chose to create us.

In the second option, God could have created a world in which created beings do not have any choices. There is no free will because God pre-programs all human decisions inside of them.

---

[132] I'm thinking of William Lane Craig, Alvin Plantinga, Roger Penrose, Richard Swinburne, Marilyn McCord Adams, and Robert Adams to name a few.

[133] Someone might ask: Could God create beings without moral free will? Of course he could. In fact, he did. We call them, "Animals." Contrary to what cat people would have us believe, a world full of amoral animals would not be satisfying as world in which moral human beings exist.

This is the Robot-World option. Interestingly, we humans have the ability to create robots like this. Though robots are handy for some tasks, we do not (or at least should not) pick them for our intimate relationships. Creating a robot wife with a "kiss me" button would hardly be as satisfying as marrying a loving woman who freely chooses to kiss you when you arrive home from school or work. We know that programming robots to love us does not produce the kind of satisfaction that we feel when a free-willed human being does. This is why despite having the technology to do so, we do not marry robots. As brilliant as we are for figuring this out, I feel God knew this long ago. That's why he did not go with option two.

Thirdly, God could have created a world with free creatures but limit the harm or good they could incur. It is like a situation where you place someone in a small, isolated room and give them the "liberty" of choosing trivial things: boxers or briefs; Coke or Pepsi; Mac or PC; Nike or Adidas; etc. The people in the room may have choices, but other than the Mac or PC decision, they do not really matter. Knowing that human history is full of great acts of good but also horrendous evils, it is evident that God did not go with option three either.

Lastly, God could have decided to create a world where humanity's free choices have the power to do great good or great evil. Increased consequences come with increased responsibility. If people could love deeply, then they could also hate or hurt deeply. If they could do exceedingly great things, then they could also be free to choose to do terrible things as well. If they could figure out a way to capture the power of an atom, then they could also find a way to make a bomb out of it.

These human beings could grow in either virtue or vice. They could learn to grow strong in faith or degenerate into weakness and anxiety. They could make difficult decisions that show charity, tolerance, justice and peace for all. Of course, if these virtues are really to be virtues at all, then the alternative of intolerance, injustice and war would have to be made possible choices as well. People get to choose to love each other, but they could also reject each other. Finally, at the zenith of our choosing ability, we could also choose to love God or reject him. As we have seen in previous chapters, some choices have eternal consequences.

We see this kind of choice all throughout the Bible. Near the end of his life, Moses stood before the Israelites and called them to make a decision. They had the choice to serve God and deny him. The former led to life; the latter, to their ruin. The choice was theirs. Moses declared:

> I call heaven and earth to witness against you today, that I have set before you life and death, blessing and curses. Therefore choose life, that you and your offspring may live, loving the Lord your God, obeying his voice and holding fast to him, for he is your life and length of days, that you may dwell in the land that the Lord swore to your fathers, to Abraham, to Isaac, and to Jacob, to give them (Deut. 30:19-20).

In a heroic, defining moment in Israel's history, Moses' successor, Joshua, stood before Israel and drew a line in the sand. What would the people do with their choice? Joshua declared his allegiance to God and called the nation of Israel to do the same:

> And if it is evil in your eyes to serve the Lord, choose this day whom you will serve,...But as for me and my house, we will serve the Lord (Josh. 24:15).

As the people of Israel confirmed over and over, though we have the will to choose, we have spoiled our choices. The effects have been disastrous in society, in our families, personally, and in our relationship to God.

Our reason, experience, and the testimony of the Bible tell us that God went with option four. We could summarize by saying that God made a world where evil was *possible*. By their sinful choices, human beings are the ones who made evil *actual*. Knowing we would commit all these evils, was it still worth it for God to make the world? It seems it was. It turns out that without evil, we would not even be here to talk about it.

YOUR PART IN AN EVIL WORLD

Thanks to the work of philosophers like Gottfried Leibniz and Robert Adams, there is one other aspect to add to the world (containing evil) that God has made. It is you! Adams writes, "It is true that we would not be ourselves without many and great evils."[134] Every possible individual that exists, exists in only one actualized world. Without some acts of pain and suffering, we would simply not exist. Take, for example, the horrible reality of war. War is terrible. Far too many human lives were lost during the wars of the twentieth century. As bad as it was, many couples met during this time. Without going into too much detail, the twinkle that sparked your great-grandparent's love led to a particular set of DNA passed on to their children. Those children (your grandparents) had children (your parents) who had you. Should any circumstance be altered, if there had been no war that caused your ancestors to meet, it would have led to totally different DNA pairings. The you that is the twenty three pairs of specific chromosomes that make "you" would never have been assembled! All this DNA I talked about got passed down because the world was in the chaos of an evil war.

A great historic tragedy is a very monumental event that shaped the construction of my own particular DNA combination. My great, great grandfather was supposed to be onboard the *Titanic*. He had a ticket for it. The official family story is that one of his connecting trains was delayed, and so he missed the boat.[135] My

---

[134] Robert Adams. "Existence, Self-Interest, and the Problem of Evil." *Nous*. (Vol. 13, No. 1: March, 1979), p. 54

[135] Some would argue that my family has been missing the boat ever since.

personal theory is that he had a few too many pints in the pub that day and lost track of time. Regardless, having missed flights and appointments because of transportation issues many times in life, I can only imagine the frustration and sheer disappointment he must have felt on that beautiful April morning when the *RMS Titanic* sailed out of Southampton, England without him. Though grieved, his grief turned to joy when he eventually met my great-great grandmother in Wales. Thankfully, because he did not die like so many did on the Titanic, he was able to pair his DNA with my great-great grandmother's DNA. Together they made my great-grandma who also got married and had kids. A few generations later, I am here just as I am, a combination of Morrison and Jones DNA.

Leibniz explains this further:

> If God had thus removed sin, a very different series of things, very different combinations of circumstances and people and marriages, and very different people would have emerged, and hence, if sin had been taken away or extinguished, they themselves would not be in the world. Therefore, we have no reason to be mad...at God for permitting the sin, since they ought rather to set their own existence to the credit of this very toleration of sins.[136]

True, the world does not always work out the way we wish it would. To complain that the world is full of evil is to also complain that you should never have existed. We are sawing off the proverbial branch on which we are sitting. Our very lives are one of the positive consequences of evil. For whatever reasons God has for allowing evil, it is redeeming to think that one of his reasons is because he wanted you to exist. It is especially reassuring to know that, even though he knew you would walk away from him and contribute evils of your own, he still made you. Furthermore, through the coming and death of his Son, he

---

[136] Gottfried Leibniz. *Confessio Philosophi*. (Frankfurt am Main: Vittorio Klostermann, 1967). p128.

has made provision that your sin be forgiven, so you can spend eternity with him.

GOD'S RESPONSE TO HUMANITY'S SIN

I wish to show that one of the reasons God permits suffering and evil is because his response is far greater than anything sin or evil could produce. In fact, this very act of God put an end to the power of both sin and evil! No matter what the scope of the evil that goes on in the world, *it cannot override God's response to it.*

The crucifixion event (Jesus' death on the cross) is the greatest display of God's attributes we have ever seen. Jesus' willingness to pay the price of our sin displays God's love, grace and mercy toward his creation. Alvin Plantinga asks, "Could there be a display of love to rival this? More to the present purpose, could there be a good-making feature of a world to rival this?"[137] In order for us to see such love, grace, justice and glory on display, God would have had to allow free beings to sin. Because of Jesus, free beings can now choose to be reunited to God and enjoy eternal life with him. Heaven is the place where people who desire to live with God and enjoy him forever can live forever in perfect peace and endless joy.

CONCLUSION

Evil is a problem that has been around for a long time. As a Christian's most challenging question, it also poses a problem for every other worldview. I have argued that, to whatever degree evil is manifest in the world, it is not contradictory to the existence of God. We must also remember that it is the choice of free human beings to commit the abundance of evils we observe in the world. This is what the logic looks like:

---

[137] Alvin Plantinga, "Supralapsarianism: O Felix Culpa." www.philosophy.nd.edu/people/all/profiles/Supralapsarianism.pdf. Accessed March 19, 2012.

1. An all-powerful, all-knowing and all-good God created the world.
2. God created a world containing evil *and has his own good reasons for doing so.*
3. Therefore, the world contains evil.

Logic is never satisfying when you are in the middle of something difficult. For a worldview to really hold up, it must be intellectually reasonable and still existentially satisfying. It must permeate your head but also reach your heart. The question for us now is: does Christianity work when you are really suffering and need it the most?

This is what we will cover in the next chapter.

WHERE IS GOD WHEN IT HURTS?:
FINDING LIGHT IN OUR DARKEST DAYS

"The gods justified human life by living it themselves, the only satisfactory response to the problem of suffering."

-Friedrich Nietzsche

Why do people *really* give up on God? In my experience, it is because of pain. Not someone else's pain - it's their own pain. When American pollster, George Barna, asked people, "If you could ask God one question and knew he would give you an answer, what would you ask?" The top response (17%) was, "Why is there so much pain and suffering in the world?"[138]

Even though tsunamis, earthquakes, famines and wars can make belief in God's goodness difficult to accept, observation tells me

---

[138] From The *OmniPoll* conducted by Barna Research Group, Ltd., January 1999.

it's the broken relationships, death of loved ones, prolonged singleness, sudden illnesses and car accidents that are the real life events that seem to break people's faith in God's goodness.

The often quoted C.S. Lewis was a man who understood pain. At least he thought he did when he was younger. Lewis lost his mother at the age of nine, was injured while fighting in the First World War and even lost his best friend in battle. Lewis felt he had experienced enough loss to write a book on the topic of suffering. In his early work, *The Problem of Pain*, Lewis defends the biblical position that evil could exist and God could still be powerful, loving and good. Lewis had his philosophical response to evil nicely covered. This was, of course, all before he lost his sweetheart, Joy Davidman. It was this tremendous grief that shook Lewis' once sound philosophical convictions. After losing Joy to cancer, nothing seemed to make sense to him anymore. Their story is always moving to me. I think it is worth sharing.

Clive Staples Lewis is remembered by friends and family as a genuinely loving human being. He was a man dedicated to academia and yet always gave priority to relationships. Lewis was the true gentleman scholar. He felt it was his Christian duty to personally respond to all mail correspondence he received. Lewis was particularly drawn to one correspondent, a feisty American woman named Joy Davidman. A long-time fan of Lewis' writing, Joy was very excited to get the chance to finally meet Lewis one afternoon in England. Escaping an abusive marriage, Joy eventually moved her boys across the Atlantic Ocean to have a new start in a town just outside of Oxford known as Headington. Joy and "Jack" (as C.S. Lewis' friends knew him) became close friends. They shared a love of literature, culture, nature, and life in general. From everything I have been told about Joy, she would have made every moment of the old British academic's life more interesting. Suddenly, their jovial time together was in jeopardy of being cut short. Joy and the boys were threatened with deportation to the USA. Heroically, C.S. Lewis, the perennial bachelor, gave her a chance to extend her stay by offering to enter into a civil marriage agreement with her. Joy agreed, and the two were married (at least in the eyes of the English government) at Oxford's City Hall. This union would be the purest form of "friends with benefits." That is, they were "just friends", and Joy had all the benefits of staying in England with her boys.

It wasn't until Joy was diagnosed with cancer a short time later that Jack realized he saw her as much more than just a friend. Mutually consenting to enter into a religious marriage, Jack arranged for his local Anglican vicar to hold a ceremony in Joy's hospital room. Thankfully, Joy's cancer went into remission, and she was released to move in with Lewis! For the next three years, the old Oxford scholar enjoyed some of the happiest times of his life.

I once had the privilege of meeting Joy's son, Douglas, who recounted the laughter the two enjoyed during this time. They went on several trips together, and Joy turned the house of Jack and Warnie (Jack's brother and lifelong roommate) from a dingy, smoke-filled bachelor pad into a warm and loving country home. Joy was true to her namesake and brought exceeding joy into Jack's life.

Sadly, Joy's cancer returned. She became bed-ridden and passed away shortly after. Lewis was heartbroken. His account of his struggles with God are written in his short book, *A Grief Observed*. Here, Lewis is honest about his struggle with God and the hurt he experienced when God took Joy away. The man who once wrote the book on the problem of pain was now without explanations. "Where is God?" Lewis cries out. "Go to him when your need is desperate, when all other help is in vain, and what do you find? A door slammed in your face."[139]

In the previous chapter I showed how it can be useful to rationalize the Christian response to suffering. We learned that

---

[139] C.S. Lewis. *A Grief Observed*. (New York, NY : HarperCollins, 1961).

what is called a "problem" with evil is actually more of a mystery than a logical contradiction. That is, our suffering does not disprove God's existence at all. People get that part wrong all the time.

I do not claim to understand God's mysterious workings. From cover to cover, the Bible reveals a God who works with people in many different wayↄ. He can never be nailed down to formulas, principles or syllogisms. At times, he blesses people who are faithful to him. Sometimes he chooses to bless people who are completely unfaithful to him. God may allow some of his saints to become extremely prosperous - but he may also allow others to suffer tremendously.

Let's examine the personal aspect of the distinctly Christian response to evil and suffering. Now we are taking off our philosophical hats and discussing this as fragile human beings- human beings who hurt and wonder "Why?" or "For how long?"

Here I want to show why Christianity's response is more personally satisfying than the atheistic or Eastern alternatives. Christianity takes the reality of evil seriously. It also affirms the goodness of God while maintaining that he is still supremely powerful.[140]

1. EVIL IS REAL AND EVIL IS WRONG

As mentioned in the last chapter, the presence of evil in the world is a problem to all world views. No worldview gets away without having to give some explanation for what evil is and how to deal with it. Though it remains a mystery how evil entered the world, the Bible never denies that it is there, that it holds significant power and that things should have been otherwise.

---

[140] For this framework I am indebted to Dr. Os Guinness and his lecture at Wycliffe Hall on November 23, 2011.

Passages like Ezekiel 28:11-19 and Isaiah 14:12-17 give us insight into the origin of evil. These passages have taught throughout church history that Satan was an angel who chose to rebel against God. He chose to set up a kingdom set against God's created order rather than submit to it. There is evil in the world not because God created it but because Satan and others have chosen to deviate from what God would want them to do.

The Genesis 1 account of creation contains the chorus, "And God saw that it was good." God's good creation was compromised by a cancer that would spread into our lives leading to broken relationships, miscarriages, illnesses, and death (to mention just a few). As Christians, we can be mad at evil and are even encouraged to fight against it. Our battle, the Apostle Paul says, "is against the cosmic powers over this present darkness... against the spiritual forces of evil" (Eph. 6:12). God knows that we get hurt by these forces. The Bible says he hears the cries of the hurting (Ex. 2:24, Ps. 34:17-18, Psalm 40:1).

The Christian worldview is not about dismissing or ignoring evil. It looks it in the face and responds to it. I do not see such an equal reaction in other worldviews. I have already talked about how I question the foundation of an atheist's claim to call something "evil." I now want to look at why I do not agree with how Eastern religions, such as Buddhism and Hinduism, approach the topic of evil.

The Eastern Response to Evil

I agree with Eastern religion's acknowledgment of the existence of suffering, pain and tragedy as an unavoidable aspect of the human experience. *Dukkha*, the first noble truth of Buddhism, is the acknowledgment that this world is broken and that living in it is a struggle. The goal, then, is to distance yourself from the pain. Pain is the result of being too attached to things of this world. Taking our introductory story for example, the Eastern religions would say C.S. Lewis only mourned over the death of his beloved, Joy, because he cared about her too much. He was too attached to earthly love and romance. Mourning is a sign of a lack of nirvana, a state of blissful, unattached enlightenment. *Karma*, another Eastern idea, is a terrible belief system for anyone who is suffering. Karma tells us that your disease or tragedy is the outworking of some wrong you have done either in a past life, or the getting of what you deserve from this one. Karma is great when you find ten dollars in your pocket but offers nothing to console a mother who loses her son to drunk driving.

Eastern concepts of reality also affirm *pantheism*, the belief that *everything* is God. The flower is god, the water is god, the sun is god and you, too, are part of god. Pantheism does not work because everything cannot be God if you want to call things "evil." The reason why we separate the creator God from his creation is because it separates God from the evil we see so prevalent in the world. If everything were God, then tragedies like the Holocaust could not be called "evil"; they would have to be called "God." Pantheism is not so much wrong as it is out of date.[141] That is, there was a time when everything was actually God, but then God created the world, and now there is a distinction between God and that which he has made. Evil is not a part of his good creation. Evil is a human-chosen corruption of God's natural order. It is not intrinsically part of it.

2. GOD IS GOOD AND HE HAS THE SCARS TO PROVE IT

If God is separated from the evil that is so prevalent in the world, what kind of a tyrant would he be to allow it to happen on his watch? Does God get any pleasure in watching people suffer? These questions raise concerns about the character of God. Is he the kind of God you can trust? This was what C.S. Lewis struggled with while grieving the loss of Joy. It was not God's existence that troubled Lewis; it was what he was like that was cause for most concern:

---

[141] C.S. Lewis. *The Problem Of Pain*. (New York, NY.: Harper Collins, 1940).

Not that I am (I think) in much danger of ceasing to believe in God. The real danger is of coming to believe such dreadful things about him. The conclusion I dread is not 'So there's no God after all,' but 'So this is what God's really like. Deceive yourself no longer.'[142]

What kind of a God could allow so much pain to run rampant in his created world? Does he sit in heaven and laugh at us when we suffer? What is God like? I learned a helpful object lesson while playing hockey at Oxford.

People are always surprised to find out that Oxford University has an ice hockey team. I was as well. When I found out about the team, I immediately signed up for tryouts. My first week in Oxford, I met Gino Bruni, the Canadian captain of the *Oxford Blues Mens Ice Hockey Club*. Gino made it clear from day one that the sole aim of the entire hockey season at Oxford was to win one game — the annual *Varsity Match* against the University of Cambridge. Our team was part of a rivalry between these two universities that goes back to the thirteenth century. Since Cambridge had won the previous year, Gino was determined to ensure our squad won the year that he was running the team. As our leader, he made us work hard, much harder than I would have liked. Regardless of the abysmal English weather conditions, we ran sprints, did circuit training and devoted valuable on-ice practice time to conditioning. Though I may not have always appreciated what he asked me to do, Gino earned my respect because he always did the training with us. I could hardly complain about the workload to the leader who was clearly working much harder than I was.

I am proud to write that the following March, in front of a sold out crowd at the Oxford Arena, we demolished Cambridge 17-1.

---

[142] C.S. Lewis. *A Grief Observed*. (New York, NY : HarperCollins, 1961).

I will not include how many goals I personally scored for I am far too modest for such a boast.[143]

My Oxford hockey training experience was more manageable knowing my leader was there to encourage me, not from the bleachers but by my side. Gino is a reflection of what Jesus does with us in our suffering. One important aspect of the Christian response to suffering is that God is a God who not only suffers himself but is with us in our suffering. I have been told that the most comforting words in the English language are, "Me, too." Did you know that God "me too's" with us when we suffer?

The God Who is Familiar with Suffering

Seven hundred years before Jesus was born, God told the prophet Isaiah that the promised Messiah was going to be a "suffering servant." He would be "pierced for our transgressions" and "crushed for our iniquities". He would endure severe punishment, but through his punishment would come the healing of the world (Isa. 53:5). God told Isaiah that God was coming to suffer.

Jesus was a Messiah who experienced human suffering in the form of hunger, thirst, sadness, injustice, betrayal, and mockery. Jesus also knew what it felt like to lose a loved one. He understood what it felt like to be misunderstood by his own family. He lived in poverty without a home of his own and travelled around as a poor, itinerant preacher. Jesus, fully God and yet fully human, was familiar with our sufferings.

Jesus knew physical suffering. He was whipped, slapped, spat on, had his beard pulled out, and then was hung to die on a Roman cross. It was not only emotional or physical pain that Jesus suffered. He experienced the spiritual pain and heartache that exacerbated his sufferings.

---

[143] The answer is three. I scored three goals.

On the cross he cried out his question, "Why have you forsaken me?" During this time God the Father was pouring out the wrath for the sin of the world on his Son. This means that the holy, perfect Father turned his back on Jesus, the one with whom he had shared eternity past. Jesus took the problem of evil upon himself, being cursed by the curse we deserve (see Gal. 3:13).

I have heard that the famous Russian novelist, Fyodor Dostoyevsky, once stared at a picture of Jesus dying on a cross for four hours. His response was this: "I don't know the answer to the problem of evil, but I do know love." When we look at the cross, we see what Jesus was willing to do in order to end the power of evil in the world. Whatever God's answer is to the existence of why we have evil, the cross is a clear demonstration that it is not for any lack in his supreme goodness.

Christians acknowledge the existence of evil as a force at work against the goodness of God's creation. Jesus Christ, who is God in human flesh, has shown us that God is indeed good and that he cares about us so much that he voluntarily suffers with us. He is not a deistic god, content to play a harp in the clouds while his creation cries out in peril. We worship a God who rolls up his sleeves and gets his hands and feet dirty in our human mess.

Thus far we have seen that the Christian response is not that God ignores evil nor that he does not care about it. That leaves us, lastly, with the question of God's power. Does God allow evil simply because he cannot stop it?

3. GOD IS POWERFUL AND HAS PROVEN IT

I can imagine that in the days between the crucifixion and resurrection Sunday, the disciples would have had a hard time trusting God's power. After three years of public ministry, Jesus was tried by the Jewish leaders and then executed by the Romans. To his disciples, the Messianic dream was seemingly lost. In the days of first-century Palestine, many would-be Messiahs talked a good game, and when the going got tough, they died. The hype of their claims and the crowds that followed them eventually faded into oblivion. We get a glimpse of this beginning to happen with two of Jesus' disciples as they walked along a road to a town called Emmaus (Luke 24). These discouraged disciples were walking home, discussing the events of Jesus' recent death. They were met along the road by one whom they deemed to be a "stranger." They openly shared their frustration with this newcomer on the journey:

> [Jesus] was a prophet, powerful in word and deed before God and all the people. The chief priests and our rulers handed him over to be sentenced to death and they crucified him; *but we had hoped that he was the one who was going to redeem Israel"* (Luke 24:20–21, emphasis mine).

Their tone from this part of the story is of two men in despair. They had put all their hope in Jesus. Now he was dead. Was it all wasted? Evil seemed to have won. This is the very real human expression of anguish that people go through when they are in pain. They cry, they lose heart, they fight, and they question God. God can take it. He is alright with us wrestling with him. We see that Jesus was patient with these disciples on the road to Emmaus. He gave them the information they so desperately needed that day.

We will return to this story in a moment. For now I want to share one of the most helpful analogies I have ever heard when it comes to working through this process of learning to trust a powerful God even when you do not understand what he is doing in your life.

The Resistance Leader Knows Best

Picture yourself in a bar in Belgium during World War 2. The Germans have invaded, and now they have control of your country. Your grief over the loss of loved ones, property and freedom have brought you to the bar on this night. You feel powerless to do anything. You order a drink as you wonder if there is anything you can do to make things right again. Down the bar from you is a middle aged man dressed in civilian clothes. He is sitting on a stool, elbows on the bar and leaning over his drink. He looks over at you and with a grizzled voice asks you, "Want to join the resistance, kid?"

How did he know that? You have only heard the stories of heroism from the battlefield. You wanted to be a part of it but were never given an opportunity. You look over at the stranger and respond hesitantly,

"Actually, yeah, I really do want to join."

He comes over and sits closer. He shows you his badge and informs you that he is a high ranking officer for the Allies. What is he doing here? He is leading a resistance as an Allied spy, infiltrating the German ranks. Tomorrow he will be putting on a Gestapo outfit and will be found among the ranks of the German army. He gives you some instructions on how you can get involved, who you need to talk to, and even offers some words of advice. Before getting up, he pauses and looks you straight in the eye. It is a moment you will not forget:

> Look, kid, it could get weird from now on. You will see me behind enemy lines, and I may be doing some things that do not make sense to you. When the war is over, we can meet here again, and I will explain it all to you. For now, you need to trust me on this one. Can you do that?

Slowly, you nod your head. Without another word, he finishes his drink and walks out.

The story of the resistance leader is an allegory about what God asks of us. God has shown us what team he leads. The Bible says, "If God is for us, who could be against us?" (Rom. 8:31). The answer is "Nobody." God tells us in the Bible what he is like. He is full of love for us. He has sent his Son to save us - what more could he do? (Rom. 8:32) He tells us that this world is not as it should be; that there is a rebellion going on, but that he is at work making it all right again. He now invites us to be a part of the resistance. During this time he will do whatever is best and has promised ultimate victory for his side. God has told us this much for sure. What we do not know now, he will explain later.[144] I cannot wait for that moment when history is explained by the author himself! I echo the heart cry of Ivan in *The Brothers Karamazov* when he says, "I want to be there when everyone suddenly understands what it has all been for."[145]

THE HOPE FACING JERUSALEM

We now turn back to Luke 24. From hope to despair, the two disciples on the road to Emmaus were discouraged over their failed hope in Jesus as a trustworthy Messiah. They soon discovered the stranger they encountered was actually Jesus (now very much alive). He showed them what he had been up to all along. He was no longer just a stranger on the road to them - he was the resurrected Messiah who walked alongside them!

> And he said to them, "O foolish ones, and slow of heart to believe all that the prophets have spoken! Was it not necessary that the Christ should suffer these things and enter into his glory?" And beginning with Moses and all the Prophets, he interpreted to them in all the Scriptures the things concerning himself (Luke 24:25-27).

What an amazing Bible study that must have been! As it turns out, Jesus *is* the one who was going to redeem Israel after all. It's just that he is doing it in a way that we did not understand.

---

[144] In a class lecture at Wycliffe Hall at the University of Oxford, Os Guinness sourced this analogy as original to Basil Mitchell.

[145] Fyodor Dostoevsky. *The Brothers Karamazov.* (New York, NY : North Point Press, 1990).

How do we know that God is powerful? By his resurrection, Jesus defeated death, that great achilles heel that has menaced human beings since the beginning.

We can easily put ourselves into this story as well. We are not just standing on the road, but we are all walking somewhere. We are facing either one of two destinations: Emmaus or Jerusalem. Facing Emmaus, we go through suffering and things are bleak. There is no hope awaiting us in Emmaus. God is dead. Death wins. There is no hope in Emmaus nor for those who are facing death. However, make a 180 degree turn, and Jerusalem is now in sight. But Jerusalem tells us that suffering, pain and death are all very real parts of the human experience. Jerusalem also tells us that God is real; that his Spirit is with us, and his victory over sin is also very real. In Jerusalem, there is an empty tomb that assures us of the power of the God who defeated his enemies: Satan, sin and death.

He will make everything new one day (Rev 21:5). He will create a New Heaven and a New Earth. We will be given new bodies. These bodies will never get sick, feel hurt, or experience sin:

> God himself will be with them as their God. He will wipe away every tear from their eyes, and death shall be no more, neither shall there be mourning, nor crying, nor pain anymore, for the former things have passed away (Rev. 21:1-4).

Heaven will be beautiful. There is no sunset, riverbank, or mountain range that could compare with images of heaven. C.S. Lewis has scratched the itch of desire for such a place that lies deep within readers of all ages. In his children's epic, *The Last Battle,* Lewis effectively connects the wonders of heaven as they outshine the greatest of earth's joys. Describing what it is like in Aslan's Country, Lewis writes:

> What was the fruit like? Unfortunately no one can describe a taste. All I can say is that, compared with those fruits, the freshest grapefruit you've ever eaten was dull, and the juiciest orange was dry, and the most melting pear was hard and woody, and the sweetest wild strawberry was sour. And there were no seeds or stones, and no wasps. If you had once eaten that fruit, all the nicest things in this world would taste like medicines after it.[146]

Pain on this side of heaven is good for us. It reminds us that we are not made just for this Earth. This world full of broken relationships and broken bodies is not our home. One day we will experience the joys of heaven. When we are caught up in moments like what Lewis just described, all of earth's troubles will seem like our faintest childhood memory.

Reflecting on the coming heaven is how the people of the Bible dealt with their worst days. They remembered that their best days still awaited them one day. Paul said, "this light momentary affliction is preparing for us an eternal weight of glory beyond all comparison" (2 Cor. 4:17). We know that Paul's afflictions were anything but easy. In the light of his home in heaven, they were light, bearable and temporary.

CONCLUSION

Suffering is like a weekend. You are either in the middle of it, about to go into it, or you are just coming out of it. My hope is that you are now better prepared for when suffering comes your way. These past two chapters serve as the best explanation I have been able to give to a problem that has at times shaken my faith and the faith of many others like me. I see now that the presence of evil does not disprove God. My experience of evil can cloud

---

[146] Lewis, C.S. *The Last Battle*. (New York, NY.: HarperCollins, 1956). p228.

my vision of God but, if I am honest, I see how pain has always brought me closer to God, not away from him.

The Christian response to evil and suffering is both intellectually reasonable and existentially satisfying. That is, it appeals to both our logic and our heart. I'm glad it includes both. If your friend is sick and dying, the most important thing is not to give them a chapter with answers in the form of philosophies and words. Logic is important, but in the presence of someone who is grieving it is best to leave the philosophy textbook behind and just sit with them, being silent, and giving them the gift of your presence.

In that way, God has shown us that he still knows how to deal with this tough subject better than all of us. Jesus promised, "I am with you always" (Matt. 28:18). He came to earth, and by the comfort of his Spirit, promised to always be here with us. In light of this, may he always be enough.

CONCLUSION:
THE BEAUTY OF A MESSENGER'S FEET

How beautiful upon the mountains are the feet of him who brings good news, who publishes peace, who brings good news of happiness, who publishes salvation, who says to Zion, "Your God reigns"

-Isaiah 52:7

After years of fighting with the Philistines, God's people are becoming battle weary. The soldiers have been in military camps for months. War is depressing. They miss their families. Their families miss them. The whole nation cries out for peace.

In a unexpected change of tactics, the Philistine leaders propose a new war strategy: *You send your best guy and we will send ours.* Each side would elect one champion to fight on behalf of the their nation. The Philistines call for a man named "Goliath." He truly is a giant of a human. Goliath comes to the front line. He seems to cast a shadow over the entire Israelite army. The Philistine giant calls out to your people, "Who will challenge me?" Nobody says a word. Who would challenge him? Losing this battle would not only cost a person his life, but the war itself would be lost. A lost war meant all of Israel being enslaved. Day after day Goliath calls out to the ranks of Israel's army. He taunts the people and makes a point to slander their God.

The rumour of the brooding giant gets passed around to Israel's tribes. From village to village and in every home, you notice people are constantly talking about it. *Have you heard the Philistines have a giant?* Some say he is ten feet tall! Others have heard it was more like twelve. His reputation as a blasphemer of God spreads. "Why won't anyone stop him?" the villages murmur. "Does God not care?" Some are confident God will move; others are not as convinced. There is a lot on the line here. A defeat would mean slavery. A victory would ensure freedom. Every conversation always ends nervously, "Keep us posted on what is going on over there."

You promise that you will. That is your job after all. You are the messenger. You have the job of traveling back and forth from the military camp to the villages reporting what is going on. These days, the message is not that exciting. "No news to report," is your common refrain. Goliath still stands at the battle line; he still taunts and Israel's army still shakes. This happens every day.

But everything changed the day that the shepherd boy showed up. He was the youngest of seven brothers, one of Jesse's kids. One day, David was delivering something to his brothers when he heard Goliath shouting his usual taunts at both God and his people. David, much to your surprise, challenges the giant, picked up a slingshot and shooting a rock that hit Goliath square in the forehead. With a thud, Goliath hit the ground face down. The giant is now dead.

It was almost as if nobody believed what they had just seen. There was a hush over both sides until finally the army of Israel erupted in a cheer. The death of Goliath meant freedom for Israel. With just one shot, the war was over. God's people would not be slaves. Having witnessed this moment, you have only one thought: *The tribes must hear this!*

It is a long journey across the valley, through the creeks and over the mountains. You fall a few times, and the heat of the Middle-Eastern sun seems to be unrelenting on your skin. Your feet are cracked. They bleed. You are probably nearly dehydrated. None of this seems to matter. You have good news to proclaim. You travel from camp to camp, in all the villages reporting to everyone the good news. "The giant is dead! There is nothing to fear anymore."

The look on the faces of those you tell makes every cut or drop of sweat totally worth it. It brings you joy to tell Israelite mothers they will not have to send their sons and daughters to be Philistine slaves.

You, the messenger, just made another person's day. In the next village over you will have the opportunity to tell the good news once again.

Of course, you are tired.
Of course, you are hungry.
Of course, you miss your bed.
Of course, your feet are cracked, bruised, bloodied and dirty.
Of course, they are still beautiful.

This is the role of the messenger.

EVERY MESSAGE NEEDS A MESSENGER

As important as it was to share about a shepherd boy slaying a giant, this event was only a foreshadowing of an even greater achievement. On the cross, Jesus hung on behalf of a scared,

208

sinful people and slew the giant of sin. He did what they could not do. We will not have to live as slaves. This kind of victory must be shared.

Following his resurrection, Jesus took his disciples to the top of a mountain and gave them an assignment that would take all of history to accomplish:

> Go therefore and make disciples of all nations, baptizing them in the name of the Father and of the Son and of the Holy Spirit, teaching them to observe all that I have commanded you (Matt. 28:19-20).

The Great Commission was a fresh commission of messengers. The disciples went from there and spread the gospel throughout Asia Minor and Europe. In the book of Acts, the Apostle Paul traveled from city to city telling whoever he could about the gospel ("good news"). Sometimes he shared the message of Jesus in synagogues and other times on mountaintops. He shared with tradesmen, religious leaders and academics. Along the journey Paul was often excommunicated, beaten, shipwrecked, hungry, homeless, and arrested because of this message.

Following Paul is a long line of messengers who took the messenger role very seriously: Tertullian, Justin Martyr, Origen, Augustine, Aquinas, Anselm, Luther, Calvin, and on and on we could go through church history. These apologists devoted their lives to articulating and defending the message.

Now it is your turn. We all have work of our own to do. In his sermon, *The Weight Of Glory*, C.S. Lewis sounded a call to messengers who can articulate our reasons for the truth of Christianity. To ignore this when it is our turn would be disastrous:

> To be ignorant and simple now — not to be able to meet the enemies on their ground — would be to throw down our weapons, and to betray our uneducated brethren who

have, under God, no defense but us against the intellectual attacks of the heathen. Good philosophy must exist, if for no other reason, because bad philosophy needs to be answered.[147]

The difference between good and bad philosophy is what needs to be sorted out today. It must be done in every classroom, office, sports team and around every dinner table. God is calling you to be that person. It is the responsibility of every generation to carry the torch and defend the truth claims of Christianity. We do not want to let the message go unheralded on our watch.

Now this book is done, a new adventure begins. The victory has been achieved. Jesus is the champion. You are the messenger. You have a message of good news to share. Get out there and get your feet dirty.

Because dirty feet are very beautiful.

---

[147] C.S. Lewis. *The Weight Of Glory*. (Harper Collins, New York, 1949). p50.

APPENDIX:

GIVING YOUR LIFE TO JESUS

A book like this demands some kind of decision. You have to do something with all this information packed into each page. Was it the truth or was it a bunch of lies and myths? I can imagine by this point you are in a kind of dilemma. You are not alone in that feeling.

Sheldon Vanauken was an American scholar in the middle of the twentieth century who found a way to study English literature at Oxford University. When he moved to England, Sheldon and his wife became friends with C.S. Lewis, whose apologetic about Christianity brought Vanauken to the brink of committing his life to follow Jesus Christ. His memoirs show that making the decision was not without an intense struggle. He wrote about being caught in the middle between belief and unbelief:

> There is a gap between the probable and the proved. How was I to cross it? If I were to stake my whole life on the risen

Christ, I wanted proof. I wanted certainty. I wanted to see him eat a bit of fish. I wanted letters of fire across the sky. I got none of these. And I continued to hang about on the edge of the gap... It was a question of whether I was to accept him - or reject. My God! There was a gap behind me as well! Perhaps the leap to acceptance was a horrifying gamble - but what of the leap to rejection? There might be no certainty that Christ was God- but, by God, there was no certainty tat he was not...I could not reject Jesus. There was one thing to do once I had seen the gap behind me. I turned away from it, and flung myself over the gap toward Jesus.[148]

Vanauken has given us a very insightful admission of what goes on in our hearts once we are confronted with the evidence to trust that Jesus is who he claimed to be - that Christianity is true and worthy of our whole lives. Vanauken saw that the reasons not to believe were not so good. There was nothing behind him anymore. There was nowhere to run but into the arms of Jesus. He knew what choice he had to make. Vanauken went for it.

I *choose* to believe in the Father, Son and Holy Ghost... Christianity has the ring, the feel of unique truth. Of essential truth... But a choice was necessary... So I choose my side. Choosing to believe is believing. It's all I can do: choose. I confess my doubts and ask my Lord Christ to enter my life. I do not affirm that I am without doubt, I do but ask for help, having chosen, to overcome it. I do but say: Lord, I believe - help Thou my unbelief.[149]

Sometimes you just have to make a decision. You don't want to be the kid on the diving board holding up the line for everyone else. Sometimes you just have to jump.

---

[148] Sheldon Vanauken, *A Severe Mercy* (London, Eng.Hodder & Stoughton, 1977), p75-100.

[149] *Ibid*. p75-100.

If you, like Sheldon Vanauken are still experiencing some doubts and yet you also feel you now have enough evidence to make a decision to trust Christ, I believe today is the best day to do so. Here are four important points about what you are choosing to believe:

1. There is a God who created this world, and he has created you to be a part of it. He created you because he loves you, has a plan for your life and wants to have a personal relationship with you.

2. Though God loves us all, we do not all love him in return. Instead, we disobey him. This disobedience is a sin against God himself (Psalm 51:4). The worst news is that sin has resulted in spiritual death which has separated us from a relationship with God affecting us today and for the rest of eternity. Hell is the consequence for those who continue to live in rebellion against God, refusing to repent of their sin.

3. Though we deserve death, the gift of God is eternal life given to us through his Son Jesus Christ (Rom. 6:23). Jesus, by his own death and resurrection has paid for sin and achieved victory over death. Now, because of Jesus, we can have peace with God (Rom. 5:1). We receive this by believing Jesus is who he says he is and confessing him as our leader and Saviour (Rom. 10:9).

4. We have a choice — to continue to live in disobedience to God or obey his call to turn from our sinful, selfish ways and return to him. The Bible promises us that everyone who does this is saved from sin and has eternal life (Rom. 10:13). Romans 8:38-39 promises that nothing can ever separate us from the love of God.

If these truths have reached both your mind and heart, it is time to commit your life to Jesus. You can pray a prayer like this:

Dear God,
Thank you that you are God, that you are real, that you made me, and that you love me. I am sorry I have not loved you as I should. I have sinned against you, and I am sorry. Thank you that Jesus died to pay for all my sin. I know that, because of him, I can be forgiven. I do not want to live my life for me anymore. I want to live for you. Come into my life and help me to follow you. I will go where you want me to go and do what you want me to do. Amen.

What an amazing adventure nows lies ahead of you as you start this relationship with Jesus Christ. Going forward, I want to encourage you with three steps. One, I would strongly suggest you go tell a Christian friend about your decision. Two, be sure you get a Bible and read some of it every day. Talk to God before, during and after your reading. The Bible is his word, and he will have something to say to you. Third, attend and serve at a church that loves Jesus, tells others about Jesus and teaches the Bible. This is such an important part of being a disciple of Jesus - being a part of his people, the church.

It's time to go get your feet dirty.

PRAISE FOR APOLOGETICS CANADA

"Apologetics Canada has not only been a wonderful organization to work with but is clearly meeting a significant need in our churches and culture to know and defend the truth that is found in Jesus Christ."

-Dr. William Lane Craig, Professor Talbot Divinity School

"I have been consistently impressed with the work of Apologetics Canada. This organization has developed and nurtured a relationship with local churches that is both deep and sincere. The church in Canada has benefited from the diligent work of this group and is wiser, better equipped and more mature as a result. I am proud of my partnership with Apologetics Canada."

-Jim Wallace, LAPD Detective, Author of *Cold Case Christianity*

"Apologetics Canada continues to demonstrate a heart for the church and to see the gospel proclaimed and defended in Canada. It has been a pleasure to work with them and we plan to continue to do so in the future."

-Jeff Bucknam, Lead Pastor, Northview Community Church

APOLOGETICS CANADA

"Challenging Thinkers to Believe and Believers to Think."

www.apologeticscanada.com

Made in the USA
Charleston, SC
10 March 2015